Transfer Pricing

Advanced Management and Accounting Series
—————————— Series Editor: David Otley ——————————

Other titles in the series

Transfer Pricing

CLIVE R. EMMANUEL
University of Glasgow

and

MESSAOUD MEHAFDI
Lancaster University

Published in association with
The Chartered Institute of Management Accountants

ACADEMIC PRESS
Harcourt Brace & Company, Publishers
London   San Diego   New York
Boston   Sydney   Tokyo   Toronto

ACADEMIC PRESS LTD.
24/28 Oval Road,
London NW1 7DX

United States Edition published by
ACADEMIC PRESS INC.
San Diego, California 92101–4311

A catalogue record for this book is available from the British Library

ISBN 0–12 238330–3

Typeset by Photo·graphics, Honiton, Devon
Printed and bound in Great Britain by Mackays of Chatham plc,
Chatham, Kent

Series Editor's Preface

David Ottley
KPMG Peat Marwick Professor of Accounting
Lancaster University

A major problem for the management accounting teacher has been the selection of a suitable text for advanced courses. Although a number of very good texts exist, they typically do not include some topics that individual teachers wish to teach. On the other hand, they do include a considerable amount of material on topics that are unnecessary for a particular course. Students often feel that they have a poor deal in purchasing large and expensive texts that do not cover the whole of their course, yet include large amounts of extraneous material.

This series is an attempt to resolve this problem. It will consist of a set of slim volumes, each of which deals with a single topic in depth. A coherent course of study may therefore be built up by selecting just those topics which an individual course requires, so that the student has a tailor-made text for the precise course that is being taken. The texts are aimed primarily at final year undergraduate courses in accounting and finance, although many will be suitable for MBA and other postgraduate programmes. A typical final year advanced management accounting option course could be built around four or five texts, as each has been designed to incorporate material that would be taught over a period of a few weeks. Alternatively, the texts can be used to supplement a larger and more general textbook.

Each text is a free-standing treatment of a specific topic by an authoritative author. They can be used quite independently of each other, although it is assumed that an introductory or intermediate-level management accounting course has been previously taken. However, considerable care has been taken in the choice and specification of topics, to ensure that the texts mesh together without unnecessary overlap. It is therefore hoped that the series will provide a valuable resource for management accounting teachers, enabling them to design courses that meet precise needs whilst still being able to recommend required texts at an affordable price.

Preface

Perhaps the most complete definition of a transfer price is that it is the monetary expression of a movement of goods or services between organisational units of the same enterprise (Wells, 1968). The study of transfer pricing may therefore include economic, organisational, and behaviour aspects as well as international and/or domestic flows of goods and services. To encompass this variety of perspectives within a slim volume has proved to be no mean challenge. Nevertheless, we have tried to present a more integrated treatment of the material than is usually the case, although, of necessity, we have been selective.

Readers who favour a neo-classical economics approach will not be disappointed by the earlier chapters on "Profit allocations?" and "Perspectives on a solution", although even at this early stage, our bias to view transfer pricing from an organisational-behavioural perspective will be apparent. Empirical evidence is introduced in Chapter 3 for both domestic and international transfer pricing in practice. Discovering how many companies employ a cost- as opposed to market-oriented transfer price is at best of academic interest, and ignores the organisational and behavioural features which influence and are influenced by the transfer pricing system. The variety of systems indicates the complexity of our task.

Nowhere is that complexity encountered more than when examining international transfer pricing. The aims of national governments, accounting regulators and fiscal agencies are unlikely to coincide completely with those of the multinational enterprise (MNE), which will itself contain conflicting views of the roles the system may play. The effectiveness of the constraints which may be placed on MNE discretion to set transfer prices is examined in Chapter 5.

Whether the focus of attention is the giant MNE or the relatively small domestic enterprise, the managerial behaviour impact of transfer pricing cannot be ignored. The interface of transfer pricing, performance evaluation and managerial rewards explains the self-interest of divisional or subsidiary management sometimes found, with dire consequences in practice. Conflict can sometimes be the result of a forced interdependence between parts of the enterprise, but it is not necessarily harmful. In certain organisational circumstances, negotiated transfer prices may solve as well as cause conflicting managerial interests.

In Chapter 8, we attempt to bring together some of the themes by

reference to two relatively recent explanatory frameworks. These are
enriched and defined by seven interacting variables which give an
impression of the wealth of data that await collection! We do not claim
that this framework is more comprehensive and complete than others,
but it may at least provide the parameters within which future research
on these dynamic interactions takes place.

C.R. Emmanuel
M. Mehafdi

Contents

1

Profit Allocations?

INTRODUCTION

Distinguishing cost allocation and transfer pricing problems is a prerequisite understanding the complexities of valuing inter-divisional work flows.

Transfer pricing can be viewed as a part of the common cost allocation problem (Thomas, 1980). In certain circumstances, the similarities associated with the two accounting treatments of interdependence can be clearly shown. However, the degree of decentralisation allowed to divisional managers can serve to distinguish the treatments. Allocation, in the short run, will inevitably recover a given amount of common cost from a possibly changing number of divisions. Transfer pricing, on the other hand, may cause divisional and overall corporate profits to change in the short run. The impact of transfer pricing on profits can be indirect and subtle. Placed in an organisational context, the way in which transfer prices are determined and modified may have a considerable influence over customer relationships and product quality, for example. Strictly applied cost formula prices, without any appeals procedure, may result in product or service quality being lowered. Freedom to negotiate a price may cause divisional managers to engage in gamesmanship. The process of transfer pricing may help cement or destroy inter-divisional cooperation, thereby affecting profits.

In this chapter, the types of decisions that transfer pricing can influence are examined. These decisions can be broadly divided into those which are strategic, tactical, or operational. By identifying the circumstances when divisional and corporate profits change, the cost allocation and

1

transfer pricing problems can be distinguished. Fundamentally, it is the degree of freedom divisional managers are delegated which demonstrates this distinction.

THE SIMILARITIES

In one important respect cost allocation and transfer pricing can be regarded as similar. Whereas allocation spreads the given cost of a service, like central research and development, over several divisions, transfer pricing can spread a given profit over several divisions. Both are mechanisms by which to trace costs or revenues to distinct segments of the business enterprise. Also, being internal to the firm, the choice of allocation base and transfer price is unfettered by legislative, fiscal or other external forces. IAS 14 (IASC, 1981) recommends disclosure of the pricing basis of inter-segment sales and transfers for distinct geographic and line-of-business segments. The British standard (SSAP 25 – ASC, 1990) does not require the basis of inter-segment pricing to be disclosed and, in fact, all EC companies can avoid segmental disclosure requirements if, in the opinion of the directors, disclosure would be seriously prejudicial to the interests of the company. The influence of fiscal and other pronouncements is questioned later, when the international dimension of transfer pricing is examined.

Furthermore, top management has a high degree of discretion as to which internal services and product flows are subject to cost allocations or transfer pricing. Attempting to distinguish the two treatments is further blurred when it is recognised that transfer prices can be cost-based. What is the difference between a budgeted, fully absorbed manufacturing cost transfer price and a predetermined overhead cost allocated to the divisions using a central service? Under either treatment, will not total company profit remain the same?

Let us take a hypothetical case, Indistinct plc, to illustrate the similarity argument. Sequential interdependence is assumed (Thompson, 1967) – that is, the output of one division becomes the input for a sister division. The receiving or transferee division then sells to independent, external third parties. The accounting numbers are purely for illustration at this stage and actuals are assumed to be known with certainty.

Company profit is £40 for each completed unit sold. Different transfer

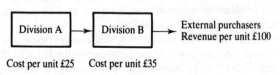

FIGURE 1.1 Indistinct plc

prices will allocate different profits to the two divisions, as shown in Example 1.1.

EXAMPLE 1.1

Profit allocations

Profit results:

Transfer price	Division A	Division B	Company
£50	50 − 25 = 25	100 − (50 + 35) = 15	25 + 15 = 40
£65	65 − 25 = 40	100 − (65 + 35) = 0	40 + 0 = 40
£25	25 − 25 = 0	100 − (25 + 35) = 40	0 + 40 = 40
£45	45 − 25 = 20	100 − (45 + 35) = 20	20 + 20 = 40

Regardless of transfer price, total company profit remains unchanged. If, instead of a transfer price, the total costs of A's operations were recovered against Division B, company profits would remain the same at £40 per unit.

However, there are certain necessary conditions for this to hold. Firstly, there is only one transfer price which represents the revenue for the supplier or transferor division and coincidentally, the cost for the transferee. In practice, this is commonly the case (Mehafdi, 1990) although it does not have to be (Fremgen, 1970).

Secondly, the internal trade or flow must actually occur. This can be achieved by top management dictat, or because the divisions have independently agreed to trade internally. These represent the extremes of the firm's attitude to decentralisation.

Thirdly, the freedom to choose alternatives to internal trade may be influenced by issues other than corporate policy. For example, the unit traded is not available externally because it is a specially designed part; or similar parts may be available, but the transferor's output incorporates 'state-of-the-art', sensitive technology involving considerable investment expenditure. Alternatively, neither division may be able to convince external purchasers or suppliers that the top management of Indistinct will not at some stage simply mandate internal trade. In addition, the number of potential suppliers and their position in the market, the number of customers and the supplier's scarce or slack capacity and the importance and uniqueness of the intermediate product or service to the supplier's core activity may be influential considerations. Freedom to choose alternatives may be constrained when, for example, a transferee division cannot obtain the large quantities required from external suppliers in order for this to become a feasible alternative to the internal trade. These conditions combine to illustrate the range of potential decisions which influence whether the internal trade will take place.

RANGE OF DECISIONS

For the trade to occur, the transferor must be capable of supplying at least the needs of the transferee. Presumably the necessary investment in human and physical resources has been undertaken to allow this. When the investment is in specialist resources, however, top management may require that internal trade takes place. In other words, when specialist equipment or skills are developed in one division to improve service to another or other divisions, decentralisation may be curtailed. The investment decision may consciously lead to goods and services being produced which have certain unique properties which are not available from any other supplier.

This strategic element of transfer pricing is sadly overlooked in the literature, and yet it is clearly an important practical issue. In our experience, there are isolated instances where the capital investment in one division has been undertaken on condition that transferee divisions will trade internally for a future, set period of time. Sometimes, the transfer price or the formula for transfer pricing is included in this contract; on other occasions a more informal, unofficial arrangement is made. An interesting research question is whether the transfer price represents cash flows to be included in the investment appraisal.

At a tactical level, whether the internal trade occurs will depend on external alternatives being available and alternative uses of internal resources and corporate policy. This is the 'make-or-buy' or 'sell-or-process further' decision.

Depending on a corporate policy of decentralisation, divisional managers may seek alternative suppliers for inputs, or alternative markets for existing outputs. Equally importantly, divisional managers may be able to switch resources previously earmarked for internal trade to other goods or services. The feasibility of these courses of action will depend on external factors also, such as the size of the internal trade relative to the external market, the unique properties of the work flows, and the sensitive technology incorporated in the transfers. Nevertheless, there may be sound reasons for external trade to be favoured by a divisional manager.

When internal trade takes place, the operational decision as to volume or quantity to transfer remains. Different transfer prices may create different levels of demand, which at one extreme may result in the transferee seeking alternative suppliers and the transferor switching internal resources to other uses. Corporate policy, the freedom and practical feasibility of the alternatives available to divisional managers, will again be influential in determining the outcome of this decision.

Hence, the motivation underlying investment decisions, the delegated decision-making of divisional managers and the practical feasibility of external trade can all influence the terms under which the internal trade, ultimately, will or will not occur. Transfer pricing, even in the domestic environment, therefore has strategic, tactical and operational dimensions. The analysis is further complicated by the chosen transfer price influencing the evaluation of investment decisions, influencing divisional managers' motivation and decision-making because of the impact on profit performance measures.

In a perfect world, the relationship between the strategic, tactical and operational decisions should be rational. For example, if investment in specific assets takes place, the output will be somewhat unique, alternatives will not be available and an agreement to trade a set quantity internally seems sensible. However, transfer pricing is applied in the multi-divisional company where swift response to changing and diverse sub-environments is of paramount importance (Emmanuel, Otley and Merchant, 1990). Each division will have a different set of internal and external alternative uses for that division's resources, which constantly change. Each division being multi-product means that outputs may be switched to or from a variety of geographic markets. Different divisional managers will, at the same point in time, hold diametrically opposite views on how best to use their resources. For one manager, the benefits may lie in pursuing the internal trade, but others may demonstrate that external alternatives are preferable.

The reality underlying the apparent stable relationships outlined in Figure 1.2 is that many markets, investment assets and products and services make up a single division. Each is subject to change, but not necessarily at the same rate or to the same extent as a sister division. Inter-divisional relationships can therefore be complicated and can generate

FIGURE 1.2 Range of transfer pricing divisions

conflict because individual managers and divisions are assessed on separate measures of profit performance. The "make-or-buy" or "sell-or-process further" decision clearly illustrates the influence of transfer pricing on corporate and divisional profits. It is on this decision that we now concentrate.

THE "MAKE-OR-BUY" DECISION

The make-or-buy decision is not only a useful example of the degree to which decentralisation may be applied, but also serves to illustrate the more strategic integration versus diversification issue. Under an organisation failures framework analysis, forward or backward integration can be upheld in terms of reduced transaction costs (Spicer and van Ballew, 1983). Imperfections in the market mean that including the product, process or service within the firm has real economic benefits. Diversification by means of expanding into different product markets, technologies, services and geographical locations reduces risk and dependence on a single core activity. Over time, however, the original reasons for these policies change, and divisions which traditionally traded extensively together may engage in less frequent transactions, whilst others may recognise mutually acceptable opportunities. The whole set of inter-divisional relationships may become more fluid as the environments faced by the divisions change.

Table 1.1 attempts to indicate the combination of factors which determine the degree of decentralisation over the make-or-buy decision.

The extent to which there is a conscious delegation of decision-making authority to lower-level managers is a matter of degree and, hence, there are no discrete or absolute values of centralisation or decentralisation. However, at the extremes, differing working practices or policies may distinguish the terms. In the case of the make-or-buy decision, it is possible to identify certain practices which if found in reality would tip the balance towards centralisation. Similarly, and not surprisingly, the opposite attributes may indicate divisional managers as the key decision-makers.

The three practices thought important in the make-or-buy decision are the availability of alternatives and discretion, plus the headquarters' need to obtain detailed divisional data.

Available alternatives

The physical existence of alternatives to the internally traded product or service provides opportunities for divisions to transact externally. Instead of making the intermediate product or providing the service within the

TABLE 1.1 Make-or-buy decision-making

Decentralised	Centralised
Available alternatives	
External market exists	No external market
Divisional assets multi-purpose	Divisional assets specific use
Discretion	
Free to use external market	HQ permission to use market
Free to switch use of assets	HQ permission to switch assets
System flows	
Free to set transfer price	HQ set transfer price
No HQ involvement in	Divisions provide detailed
information provision	information for HQ
Decision-maker	
Divisional	Headquarters
general	Staff
manager	

multi-divisional company, these can be bought-in from external, independent third parties. It is assumed that non-price competition in the external market does not create significant imperfections.

When an external market does not exist, the divisional manager may yet have the ability to switch resources either to or away from internally traded products and services. This assumes that divisional assets are not so specific that they cannot be redeployed on existing or new product lines. Given the size and diversity of individual divisions today, the alternative use of divisional resources is a realistic possibility (Hill, 1985). When either the external or internal alternative is available, the feasibility of regularly "making or buying" the intermediate product or service internally can be questioned.

Discretion

The freedom to use an external market or to switch divisional resources is a matter of degree, usually. Some companies may only allow the alternative actions after headquarters have been consulted and permission granted. Others develop rules allowing external suppliers to be used up to, say, 30% of total requirements of a particular intermediate product or service. There is a whole spectrum of practices – as usual, a balance needs to be struck. Discretion to use an external market internalises competitive forces and provides a benchmark against which divisional efficiency can be gauged. In contrast, the benefits of integration may be reduced and sensitive information provided to competitors.

The degree to which divisional managers are given this discretion will influence the dynamic nature of the make-or-buy decision.

System flows

The ability of headquarters staff to set or arbitrate transfer prices is dependent on the amount and quality of information regularly reported by the divisions. Central information flows may yet result in overload problems, and the perception that transfer pricing is determined centrally. Without detailed information, however, headquarters staff will be unable to set relevant prices. Hence, the extent and detail of centralised information flows can influence the degree of decentralisation over the make-or-buy decision.

The importance of obtaining an effective balance between these practices in order that the make-or-buy decision is taken correctly in an economic sense is the concern of the rest of this chapter.

Let us argue that in the example of Indistinct plc, Division B can obtain external revenue of £60 by redeploying the exact same resources previously devoted to internal trade to an alternative good or service. Divisional profit becomes £25 per unit, an increase over all internal trade situations when the transfer price is greater than £40 per unit. However, the impact of B's decision on Division A is unclear.

If A can switch its resources to an alternative good or service, Indistinct's overall profit may be maintained, increased or reduced. If substitution is not possible, because the resources at Division A are very specialised, then a decline in corporate profit is to be expected.

Only top management, or a level above the divisional management, is capable of gauging the effect of this decentralised decision-making. Hence, the relevant information must flow to the centre, otherwise divisional managers who are disillusioned with transfer pricing may take decisions which increase divisional profit at the expense of corporate profit. Progressive advances in information technology enable central records to be updated and maintained quickly. Networking of decision support systems may overcome the problem of information asymmetry in large enterprises, thereby improving central decision-making. There is, however, an alternative viewpoint on the degree of decentralisation which is needed.

By allowing Division A to determine the effective employment of existing resources between alternative uses, corporate profit can increase. With Division B earning a profit of £25 per unit, A needs only to find a substitute good or service to be sold externally at £40 per unit to maintain corporate results. Using the resources previously earmarked for internal trade to provide an alternative which sells at £50 or above gives better profit results for Division A in all cases other than when the £65 transfer price operates. It is not obvious, therefore, that top management should be involved even when there are no practically feasible alternatives for the internally traded commodity but alternative uses of the divisional resources are available. Provided divisional management have the relevant information, allocated profit can be improved. As mentioned earlier, strategic management issues such as capital investment associated with the internal trade may counterbalance this, however, especially if highly specific assets are involved.

Top management dictating the inter-divisional trade results in profit allocations whether or not practically feasible alternative markets exist for the transferred good or service. When alternatives exist, however, divisional management may be able to influence the transfer price itself by admitting the pricing policies of competitors, for example, to the internal negotiations. Ultimately this may result in a redistribution of profits shown against each division, but there are the compatible dangers of phantom prices and biased market expectations being introduced. Non-price market imperfections should not be overlooked either, in that delivery, quality, guarantee/warranty factors can be influential factors. The unavailability of data relating to external equivalent goods or services allows top management complete discretion in the setting of the transfer price or the 'best poker player' to reap apparent benefits when divisional managers can negotiate the transfer price.

Where the make-or-buy decision is determined by divisional managers and alternatives are practically feasible, the elements of the true transfer pricing problem are combined. Managers have access to alternative goods or services which are equivalent to those available internally, and they have individual discretion to use those alternatives. The decision to make or buy externally may increase corporate and divisional profits or increase one division's profit at the expense of total company profit. However, there is the secondary question of how extensive the inter-divisional trade should be.

EXTENT OF INTERNAL TRADE

If Division A has the capacity to produce 100,000 units and Division B has demand for 70,000 units in a given period, Indistinct plc may face the following situations when the expected market price is (a) £40 per unit and (b) £60 per unit. Assume the mutually agreed transfer price is £45.

EXAMPLE 1.2

Expected market price: £40 per unit

(a) *With internal trade*

Division A		Division B	
Transfer price	£45	Selling price	£100
Cost	£25	Cost	£35
		Transfer price	£45
Internal 20 × 70,000 = £1,400K			
External 15 × 30,000 = £450K		20 × 70,000	£1,400K
			====
	£1,850K		
	====		

(b) *No internal trade*

Division A		Division B	
Selling price	£40	Selling price	£100
Cost	£25	Cost	£35
		Market price	£40
	15 × 100,000		
	= £1,500K		25 × 70,000
	====		= £1,750K
			====

In Example 1.2, where is the incentive, in financial terms, for Division B to buy internally? The total of divisional profits suggests that corporate profit remains unchanged, but when no internal trade takes place, is it likely that Division A can sell an additional 30,000 units externally which do not reduce the market price below £40 per unit?

EXAMPLE 1.3

Expected market price: £60 per unit

(a) *With internal trade*

Division A		Division B	
Transfer price	£45	Selling price	£100
Cost	£25	Cost	£35
		Transfer price	£45
Internal 20 × 70,000 = £1,400K			
External 35 × 30,000 = £1,050K		20 × 70,000	£1,400K
			====
	£2,450K		
	====		

(b) *No internal trade*

Division A		Division B	
Selling price	£60	Selling price	£100
Cost	£25	Cost	£35
	———	Market price	£60
35 × 100,000 =	£3,500K		———
	====	5 × 70,000 =	£350K
			====

In the situation shown in Example 1.3, why should Division A supply any of its output internally? Even if only 70% of total capacity is sold externally, this is equivalent to total divisional profit when internal trade is undertaken. As before, the market price may change when Division B seeks alternative suppliers and, perversely, the market price may rise, reducing the incentive for Division A to increase capacity utilisation.

The strength of these arguments is conditioned by the relative size of the internal to the external market and other suppliers' capacity utilisation and purchasers' demand. However, it should be apparent that profits are no longer being internally allocated, nor is total corporate profit likely to remain constant.

Giving divisional managers this degree of freedom over the make-or-buy decision has been recognised, at least, implicitly in practice. By limiting the volumes of external trade, top management may constrain the worst effect of managers pursuing individual divisional profitability. Allied Lyons, for example, allows potential transferee divisions to obtain a maximum of 15% of inputs externally. Others, like Ultramar, require internal demand to be satisfied before transferors can sell externally (Emmanuel, 1977).

Theoretically optimum solutions also recognise the potential difficulties in these situations, and in Chapter 2, the suggestions for directing divisional managers towards levels or volumes of trade in the company's best interests are explored. Suffice it, for the moment, to state that all of these solutions require centralised information flows. Not just each division's cost and revenue data are required, but schedules for different levels of activities also must be provided. This highlights the last of the necessary conditions for transfer pricing to be distinguished from cost allocations: namely, that centralisation of divisional information is not required, otherwise the ham-fisted hand of top management involvement will cause decentralised profit management to be replaced once more with profit allocations. The justification for this assumption will become clear in the next chapter.

SYNOPSIS

An attempt has been made to identify the distinctive characteristics of common cost allocations and transfer pricing. By focusing on these organisational characteristics, the strategic, tactical and operational aspects of transfer pricing are recognised. Of singular importance is the identification of the level of management which can decide whether or not the internal trade takes place. When practically feasible external alternatives exist, or when alternative uses of divisional resources are available and divisional managers are free to mutually agree to trade, corporate and divisional profits can be changed by transfer pricing. In all other cases when top management rule that the trade should occur, whether or not practically feasible alternatives exist, transfer pricing merely acts as a means for allocating profits between divisions. Corporate profit cannot be altered, except that the effect of the transfer price on divisional management performance may create opportunities for bickering, gamesmanship and conflict which may themselves alter corporate profit. Chapter 7 covers these issues in depth.

The degree of decentralisation which enables divisional managers to control the "make-or-buy" or "sell-or-process further" decisions, and to determine the quantity of internal trade, fundamentally distinguishes transfer pricing from common cost allocation. It should be highlighted that no reference to particular bases or types of transfer price has been made. This is the concern of subsequent chapters. Neither has the analysis distinguished domestic and international situations. It is believed to be relevant to both situations, but as will be shown in Chapter 4, there are additional influences to be considered in the international case.

As a result, we will next concentrate on theoretical solutions to the make-or-buy and quantity decisions which:

1. Assume that divisional management has some discretion over these decisions.
2. Assume that practically feasible alternatives exist to the internal trade.
3. Assume that centralised information flows are not required by top management.

QUESTIONS

1. Using the analysis in this chapter as a framework, identify the influences on internal trade when:
   (a) a transferor division can supply two or more transferee divisions;
   (b) a transferee division can purchase from two or more transferor divisions.

2. Recompute the effect of internal as opposed to external trade in Indistinct plc when the expected market price is £50 per unit.
   What are the implications of the transferred good or service having unique and specialised properties in this case?
3. Identify the similarities and distinguishing features of common cost allocations and transfer pricing.
4. Describe the forms of divisional management discretion which may influence the occurrence or quantity of internal trade. How might the level of discretion be limited by top management for legitimate reasons?
5. Outline the implications and potential significance of an integration as opposed to diversification strategy on transfer pricing.
6. Using the Indistinct plc example, assume that Division A is able to sell at £60 per unit and Division B can purchase at £40 per unit. What will be corporate profit? What conditions are needed for this result to be achieved?
7. How, if at all, might the strategic, tactical and operational aspects of transfer pricing interrelate?

☐ 2 ☐

Perspectives on a Solution

INTRODUCTION

A major deterrent to ensuring that divisional managers take decisions in the company's best interest is the basis on which the transfer price is determined. The transfer price represents revenue for the supplying division, and cost of an equal amount for the purchasing division, unless a dual pricing scheme is used (Adelberg, 1986; Kaplan and Atkinson, 1989). These revenues and costs vary with the quantity traded, as in any normal transaction. However, different bases of transfer pricing will influence whether or not the internal trade occurs, and at what volumes. Furthermore, the transfer price will affect the divisional profit performance measures which are used to appraise the divisional manager's performance (Vancil, 1979). A saving of a few pence on the transfer price may magnify and guarantee divisional profit or loss when significant volumes are involved.

In this chapter, the accountant's general rule for determining transfer prices, that is variable cost plus opportunity cost (Horngren and Foster, 1987) is examined. The potential for various bases accommodating this rule are investigated for domestic transfers of goods and services. In this analysis, marginal cost, full cost, shadow prices and market prices are reviewed, and their underlying assumptions are exposed. The consistency of these assumptions with divisional general managers having discretion over the make-or-buy decision, alternatives to internal trade being practically feasible and centralised flows of information being unnecessary, influence the conclusion that all are defective. An alternative organisational perspective is required, as provided by amongst others, the fair and neutral basis for calculating transfer prices.

SUBOPTIMISATION AND OPPORTUNITY COSTS

Opportunity cost is the value associated with the next-best alternative use of a scarce resource. The concept has a pedigree harking back to Ricardo, writing in the early nineteenth century about economic rent, yet it encapsulates the problem of determining the transfer price today. The key question is: "Whose opportunity cost should be included in the transfer price?"

At one level, there is the opportunity cost of the company as a whole, and at another the opportunity costs of the divisions. When practically feasible alternatives to the internal trade exist, three views on the value of opportunity cost will be available if just two divisions are involved. A simple example may illustrate this.

Division R can provide a service to an outside client for £500, less incremental costs of £90. Alternatively, another of the company's divisions, Division S, will use the service in the manufacture of Hidgets, hybrid widgets. Hidgets can be sold externally for £900, but in addition to the cost of the internal service, Division S incurs processing and marketing variable costs of £450. Division R is convinced that any internal provision of the service should be at a transfer price of not less than £600.

Being a rational, profit-motivated person, Division S's manager will decide not to purchase the service internally (loss of £150; £900 − 450 − 600). For the company, however, the opportunity cost of the internal trade is a profit of £40 (£900 − 450 − (500 − 90)). If Division R does agree to trade internally, the opportunity cost associated with the alternative of providing the service to an external client is £410 (£500–90). The £410 represents the contribution forgone in not supplying the service to the external client. Whose view is taken determines the opportunity cost.

When headquarters staff intervene and dictate a transfer price for the service of £410, Division R's opportunity cost, total profits of £40, are achieved. However, should the Hidgets' selling price fall to £750, even at the revised transfer price of £410, Division S would not want the service (loss of £110; £750 − 410 − 450). This would be an optimal decision from the company and the divisions' viewpoints, if and only if Division R was operating at full capacity. When there is spare capacity due to insufficient demand from external clients, the opportunity cost of the service is £90, the incremental cost of providing the service. Substituting this opportunity cost value, Division S finds the Hidgets profitable, £210, as would the company. The relevant opportunity cost value therefore also depends on whether the resource is truly scarce.

Applying the concept of opportunity cost is problematic, for two reasons. Firstly, the divisional and corporate managements can legitimately hold different views of the value. Secondly, in the decentralised company where divisional managers can determine alternative uses for resources, scarcity, and hence the value of the opportunity cost, can be contrived or manipulated. The practical application of the accountant's general rule that the minimum transfer price should be variable cost plus the opportunity cost for the good or service to the firm as a whole is therefore problematic. When the resource is limited or capacity is constrained, an opportunity cost equivalent to the next best alternative use – in our example, supplying the external client – is relevant. If not constrained, the variable or incremental costs incurred in supplying the service is the relevant opportunity cost. Divisional managers who control the use of resources under their command can determine the extent to which certain resources, services or goods are constrained. The general rule may guide divisional managers to make optimal decisions if the transfer price incorporates relevant opportunity costs, but the rule fails to take into account the fact that managers can control the opportunity cost by the operating decisions they have authority to take.

The incentive for managers to select carefully which mix of products or services a finite amount of resources will supply could result in transfer prices which include high opportunity cost values. For example, switching skilled labour from a product line serving internal and external customers to other lines may cause a scarcity. Redistribution of resources within the division to create these opportunity costs will enhance the profitability rating of the division and the manager. By following this policy, the divisional manager is acting rationally under a profit-responsible control system. Rather than preventing this type of behaviour, transfer prices based on the accountant's general rule may actually encourage it! Despite these shortcomings, the search for transfer prices incorporating opportunity costs continues, although there is a growing awareness of their inadequacies (Cats-Baril, Gatti and Grinnell, 1988).

If the opportunity cost element of the general rule poses difficulties, it should not be inferred that the variable or incremental cost is trouble-free. Arguments abound as to whether standard or actual cost, full cost or full cost plus should be used.

COST BASES

Basing transfer prices on standard costs has the benefit of making supplying divisions aware of costs and the need to be efficient. The use of actual costs allows the inefficiencies to be passed on without penalty. However, the standard cost of prototype, customised or unique intermediate goods may be difficult to set, and certainly for services this appears true (Gardner and Lammers, 1988; Keegan and Howard, 1988). There is the question of the bench-mark standard. Should this be based on previous years' performance of the same divisions, similar divisions or service suppliers within or outside the firm, on competitors' perform-ance or industry averages? There is also the possibility of bench-marking on the basis of similar activities undertaken in different industries (Kaplan and Norton, 1992). When the result is that standards are continually tightened, what incentive is there for supplying divisions to invest in cost-saving work practices or equipment?

The first part of the accountant's general rule is taken to refer to incremental cost as the additional outlay costs per unit incurred to the point of transfer which may be approximated by variable costs. This is only an approximation, because incremental cost can include costs other than strictly variable costs and as such, is often termed marginal cost. Solomons (1965) recognises that marginal cost has a real claim to form the basis of transfer prices, as long as there are no short-run limitations on capacity. There is also a significant collection of neo-classical economists, beginning with Barone (1938) and pursued most actively by Hirshliefer (1956, 1957), who have promoted marginal cost for this purpose.

Marginal cost

The economist's general rule is to set the transfer price at the marginal cost of the supplying division at the optimal output level. Determination of the transfer price under this approach is illustrated in Example 2.1.

EXAMPLE 2.1

Marginal cost transfer pricing

	Division X	Division Y
Average cost	$25 + 7.5Q$	$5Q$
Average revenue	—	$200 - 2Q$

Where Q represents the quantity of output

To calculate marginal cost and revenue, these continuous functions need to be converted to total costs and revenues, and then differentiated.

	Division X	Division Y
Total cost	$25Q + 7.5Q^2$	$5Q^2$
Total revenue	—	$200Q - 2Q^2$
Marginal cost	$25 + 15Q$	$10Q$
Marginal revenue	—	$200 - 4Q$

Optimal output level: MC = MR

$$25 + 15Q + 10Q = 200 - 4Q$$
$$29Q = 175$$

Optimal output level = 6.04 (approximated by 6) units

Optimal transfer price = Marginal cost of supplying division at the optimal output level

$$= 25 + 15(6) = £115 \text{ per unit}$$

The profit performance of the individual divisions becomes:

Division X

		£
Internal revenue: 115(6)		690
Total costs: $25(6) + 7.5(6)^2$		(420)
Profit		270

Division Y

Total external revenue: $200(6) - 2(6)^2$		1,128
Total costs of Division Y: $5(6)^2$	180	
Transfer price 115(6)	690	(870)
Profit		£258

Corporate profit reconciliation:

Total external revenue: $200(6) - 2(6)^2$		1,128
Total costs of Division X:		
$25(6) + 7.5(6)^2$	420	
Total costs of Division Y: $5(6)^2$	180	(600)
Total profit		£528

The figure produced (Figure 2.1) is the optimal profit for the firm and by combining the marginal revenue and marginal cost data for the purchasing division to create a net marginal revenue curve, the position can be shown in a graph. The net marginal revenue curve effectively describes the maximum amount the purchasing division has available to pay for the transferred commodity or service.

The shaded area, ABC, represents the profit of Division Y and the unshaded area, CBD, the profit for Division X. The rigour and neatness of this solution is based on several fundamental assumptions such as technological and demand independence between divisions (Hirshliefer, 1956). For our purposes, the behavioural and organisational implications of this approach are concentrated upon.

Firstly, there is an inducement for the supplying divisional manager to increase costs. Only if marginal costs are rising will a profit be shown for this division. A horizontal or declining marginal cost curve will result either in zero profit or a loss. The position for this manager deteriorates when marginal costs exclude some fixed costs. The economist's approach therefore provides an inducement for the supplying division to become cost inefficient, or to operate at a level where diseconomies of scale are encountered.

Secondly, the optimal solution is only obtained when all the relevant information is centralised. The obvious choice is that headquarters staff receive the schedules of average cost and average revenue in order to determine the optimal output level and, hence, the optimal transfer price. Alternatively, one of the divisions may act in this capacity but in this case, self-interest may prevail. In either event, the pooling of a significant amount of data from the divisions is in direct contradiction of the information economies associated with decentralisation. The "ham-fisted" hand replaces the invisible hand of market forces. By dictating either the

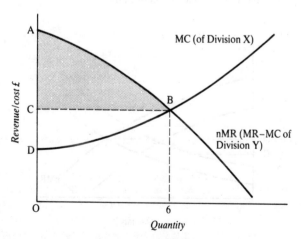

FIGURE 2.1 Optimal output and transfer price

optimal quantity or the optimal transfer price, divisions are being directed towards the corporate preferred outcome.

Thirdly, once the system of transfer price determination is known to divisional managers, can the information they provide be relied upon? Ronen (1992) suggests a truth-telling system which attains efficiency unless managers co-ordinate their messages. No way of safeguarding against this is offered, however, and managers will, by adjusting estimates of average revenue in a pessimistic way, alter the shape of the net marginal revenue curve to form a steeper decline, or a new and lower curve may be inputted to the economic analysis. Similarly, the supplying divisional manager may recognise that up-lifting average costs can be beneficial. Figure 2.2 illustrates this.

By inflating cost estimates, the supplying division can obtain a higher transfer price, TP_2, whereas under-estimation of revenue or over-estimation of costs by the purchasing division can lower the transfer price to TP_1. In both instances, the optimal output level is not achieved and corporate profit will be reduced. Preventing or even monitoring this induced behaviour would involve headquarters staff verifying the data transmitted from the divisions. This may be achieved at only some considerable cost, dependent on the number and frequency of internal trades. Again this need for verification of divisional cost and revenue estimates, which may be difficult to forecast anyway, contradicts decentralisation. How can divisional managers be held responsible for their separate profit performance when top management intervention through the setting of transfer prices is apparent?

Whilst the foregoing approach may be familiar to economists, the following example may appeal to accountants.

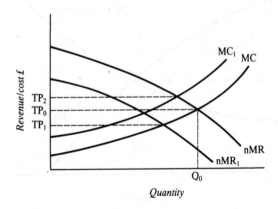

FIGURE 2.2 Impact of estimate manipulations

Incorrigible PLC has two divisions which may trade internally together. Division L's output, an intermediate part, can be converted by Division M into a saleable final product. Most of Division L's costs are fixed. At an output of 1,000 parts per day, total costs amount to £2,250 per day and increase by £600 for each additional 1,000 parts made.

Division M incurs additional conversion costs of £2,500 per day at an output of 1,000 parts and these increase by £500 for each additional 1,000 parts used. Sales of the final product are expected to take the following pattern:

Sales (units)	Revenue per 1,000 units
1,000	£3,500
2,000	£2,650
3,000	£2,300
4,000	£2,075
5,000	£1,900
6,000	£1,750

One part supplied by Division L is required to produce one final product unit.

Example 2.2 illustrates the economist's approach to the determination of the optimal transfer price in this situation.

EXAMPLE 2.2

Optimal transfer price determination

Sales / output units	Division L		Division M			
	Total cost	Marginal cost	Total own cost	Marginal cost	Total revenue	Marginal revenue
	£	£	£	£	£	£
1,000	2,250	—	2,500	—	3,500	—
2,000	2,850	600	3,000	500	5,300	1,800
3,000	3,450	600	3,500	500	6,900	1,600
4,000	4,050	600	4,000	500	8,300	1,400
5,000	4,650	600	4,500	500	9,500	1,200
6,000	5,250	600	5,000	500	10,500	1,000

Optimal output where marginal cost equals marginal revenue:
At 5,000 output: 600 + 500 < 1,200
At 6,000 output: 600 + 500 > 1,000

The optimal transfer price at the 5,000 level of output is £600 per 1,000 batch of parts giving a maximum company profit of £350. The transfer price per part is 60 pence.

Although consistent with the previous illustration of the application of the economist's approach, the same defects emerge, when viewed from an organisational and behavioural perspective:

1. Division L can never report a profit, due to the horizontal shape of the marginal cost curve and the relatively high fixed costs of this division.
2. The centralisation of information is again apparent and the need to provide cost and revenue data at all levels of operation is shown.
3. Can the data be verified in a cost-effective manner, especially when the revenues are estimates made in an uncertain, dynamic world?

Full cost basis

Reflecting the allocation debate (Zimmerman, 1979), the theoretical arguments which support marginal, incremental or variable cost transfer pricing appear to be overwhelmingly rejected in practice. There is little empirical evidence (Chapter 3) to indicate these bases are employed, and yet full cost and full cost plus transfer prices are widely used (Borkowski, 1988).

In similar vein to Zimmerman, Miller and Buckman (1987) show that allocated fixed costs can serve as a proxy for difficult-to-measure opportunity costs. The same suggestion was made by Baxter and Oxenfeldt in 1961, and which has more recently been adopted by Tomkins (1990). Using a pragmatic–analytical approach, Tomkins provides an analysis which shows that the combination of cost-plus transfer pricing and negotiation at the margin can be justified to secure shorter-run optimal decisions. Applying sensitivity analysis to assess the validity of his findings, Tomkins concludes that "near optimization can result from modified absorption costing practices" (ibid., p. 215). There are limits, however, on the proportion of contribution the supplying division is targeted to achieve and the range over which the volume of trade can be negotiated. Nevertheless, the similarity with corporate pricing practices (Silbertson, 1970) and this model suggests that further empirical research is justified.

Kaplan and Atkinson (1989) advocate activity-based costing (ABC) as an alternative to absorption costing to calculate full cost transfer prices. The ABC approach is argued to be a more accurate measurement of the economist's long-run marginal cost and the long-run variable costs needed for managerial decision-making. The distinction with Tomkins is not that full cost transfer prices are indefensible, but rather on the basis of calculation and their effectiveness in short-term or longer-term decision-making.

The explicit inclusion of negotiation in Tomkins' model uncovers a further debate: namely, will negotiation enhance conflict resolution or generate conflict? It may offer the opportunity to clarify strategic ambiguities, or to allow "the best poker player to win" (Eccles, 1985a). Recent laboratory experiments by Dejong *et al.* (1989) and Chalos and Haka (1990) suggest that the bargaining history affects profit results over successive time periods. The negotiations may improve or reduce corporate profit, but gaming did not appear to be prevalent, although conditioned by the presence of a managerial incentive scheme. Chalos and Haka therefore conclude that the operation of transfer pricing systems within the context of compensation schemes, negotiating history and intermediate market uncertainty require investigation.

The significance of the negotiation process relates to the need to provide an element of profit in addition to the full cost transfer price. Without this, there is little incentive for the supplying division to trade internally or, more importantly, to improve on the service offered to purchasing divisions. Why should the supplying division invest in cost-reducing or quality-improving equipment when the transfer price allows little or no profit to be earned? Monden and Nagao (1989) focus on the sharing of risk between suppliers and buyers by means of an analysis of expected utility. Tomkins and McAuley (1991) offer an alternative analysis through simulation, where the aim of the resulting transfer price is to create positive debates centring on divisional managers' risk.

These developments suggest that full cost and full cost plus transfer prices cannot be dismissed as theoretically unsound. When taken in an organisational context, their combined use with ABC and negotiation may offer economic and behavioural benefits which exceed the costs of the information provision. In this last respect, the low cost apparently associated with market-oriented transfer prices requires consideration.

MARKET-ORIENTED PRICES

There is one occasion when determining the transfer price has no impact on corporate profitability, even when the divisions can freely use external markets. This is when a perfectly competitive external market for the transferred good or service exists. In this instance, the market price equals the marginal cost of the supplying division, and the profit of the enterprise is unaffected whether the divisions trade internally or externally (Hirshleifer, 1956). However, the existence of perfectly competitive markets, especially for intermediate goods and services, is highly unlikely in practice (Atkin and Skinner, 1975). Imperfectly competitive markets indicate that the net price received by the selling division is different from the price which is paid by the purchasing division externally. This is due to the selling division incurring transportation costs, selling costs, marketing costs and debt collection costs which can be avoided when engaged in internal trade (Gould, 1964). The presence of these costs results in not one, but two market prices being available for transfer pricing.

Using Gould's analysis, three situations can now occur:

$$P_B > P_s > P$$
$$P > P_B > P_s$$
$$P_B > P > P_s$$

where P_B is the price facing the purchasing division in the external market; P_s is the price at which the selling division can sell in the external market; P is the optimal price determined by the economist's approach.

Figure 2.3 depicts the first of these situations.

The transfer price should be set at P_s, the price obtained by the selling division in the imperfectly competitive external market. This will induce the selling division to supply OQ_1 and earn a profit equivalent to the area 123. At this transfer price, the buying division will demand OQ_2 giving a profit equivalent to the area 345. The company improves on the economist's solution which indicates an internal trade of OQ by the profit equivalent to the area 246. However, this improved corporate position can only be attained by constraining the autonomy of the selling

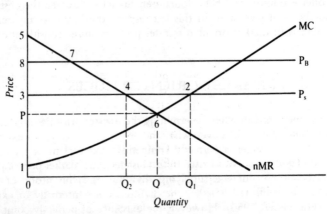

FIGURE 2.3 Transfer pricing and external markets

division, in this case. This division must be told to satisfy internal demand before selling externally. Unless OQ_2 is supplied to the buying division, the rational purchasing manager will only purchase up to point 7 at the external market price of P_B. The selling division's profit is unaffected whether OQ_1 is sold entirely in the external market or if OQ_2 is sold internally and $OQ_1 - OQ_2$ is sold externally. In the absence of any incentive for the selling division to improve the profit performance of a sister division, whose manager may be a competitor for promotion, annual rewards, etc., headquarters staff must instruct the selling division in order that OQ_2 becomes the internal trade. A similar but opposite instruction is required when $P > P_B > P_s$.

So, in addition to the centralisation of information and the potential manipulation of costs and revenues, divisional autonomy has to be constrained in order that corporate performance is improved. The relationship of P, P_B and P_s has also to be determined and finally, the value of the divisional profit performance report is compromised. Under Figure 2.3, the use of P_s as the transfer price plus corporate instruction, results in the buying division showing a profit equivalent to area 345. However, if this division is treated on a "stand-alone" basis, trading in the external market results in a profit of only 578. The ability of the divisional profit performance report to reflect separate economic viability is badly compromised. The need for corporate intervention and instruction is equally apparent when the external market is imperfectly competitive (Tomkins, 1973).

Further complications have been investigated to address oligopolistic competition (Naert, 1973) and bilateral monopoly (Chalos and Haka, 1990). The trade-off, however, remains the same: an economic optimal solution at the expense of divisional autonomy, or a sub-optimal solution which maintains divisional autonomy and, hopefully, managerial responsibility.

SHADOW PRICES

The complexity of real-life transfer pricing becomes apparent when several divisions are seen to use one or more supplying divisions, when several goods and services are internally traded and when reciprocal interdependence is present. One line of approach is to apply linear and mathematical programming, which is summarised in Abdel-Khalik and Lusk (1974), Thomas (1980) and Grabski (1985).

Again, the centralised flow of information is a prerequisite, with the primal solution of the linear programme indicating the volumes of trade and the dual solution providing values for the scarce resources. These dual values, or shadow prices, when combined with the relevant variable costs of constrained resources, can be used to develop transfer prices.

For example, if product K has variable costs of £10 related to its process of manufacture through machine 1 (30 minutes) and machine 2 (3 hours), and the dual solution indicates that machine 1 has slack but machine 2 has a shadow price of £2.08, then the transfer price for K is:

$$k = 10 + 0.5 \times 0 + 3 \times 2.08 = £16.24 \text{ per unit}$$

In turn, these transfer prices divide the overall corporate profit to each attributable division (Mepham, 1980). However, even with an iterative decomposition procedure (Baumol and Fabian, 1964; Jennergen, 1972), ultimately the divisions are informed of the appropriate transfer price and the volumes of internal trade. Further extension of these mathematical approaches to 'game-theoretic' models provides sophisticated solutions to the transfer pricing problem, but requires significant centralisation of information. Hence, the application of this approach, the economist's rule and the accountant's rule tend to transform the transfer pricing challenge into a cost allocation solution by constraining divisional autonomy. To be effective, each method requires an element of instruction from corporate management or headquarters staff and/or centralisation of information. This holds true even when it is practically feasible for divisional managers to use an external market. The distinctions drawn in Table 1.1 may be reinforced by the approach adopted for determining the transfer prices. These are shown in Table 2.1.

Certain bases are not feasible, as, for example market price when there is no external market. Marginal and shadow price approaches are only feasible if divisions provide detailed information to headquarters. When divisional managers set the transfer price, there is the possibility of negotiation over-laying the approach, whereas at the other extreme, a formula

TABLE 2.1 Contingent transfer pricing bases

Decentralisation	Centralisation
←— — — — — — — — —	— — — — — — — — — —→
Alternatives available	Unavailable
Discretion at Division	HQ permission required
No HQ involvement in	Divisions provide detailed
information provision	information for HQ
Transfer pricing bases	
Market oriented	Full cost
Pragmatic analytic full cost	Marginal cost
Negotiated	Shadow/dual prices
	Opportunity cost
	Formula determined

or centrally determined approach may be applied. The positioning of these transfer price bases is related to the three influences, alternatives available, discretion and central information requirements which it has been suggested determine the degree of decentralisation. Whilst there is considerable empirical evidence relating to practice (see Chapter 3), there is none to test specifically the relationships shown in Table 2.1. Concentration on the polar extremes ignores the vast and interesting middle ground. However, the extremes allow the age-old trade-off in transfer pricing to be seen: approaches which maintain decentralisation may allow sub-optimal decisions to be taken, and vice versa. This conundrum has led to the development of other approaches to transfer price.

FAIR AND NEUTRAL PROCEDURE

One approach worth considering is a suggestion by Emmanuel and Gee (1982) which incorporates the concept of opportunity cost but maintains divisional autonomy. To illustrate the mechanics, the Indistinct plc case in Chapter 1 will be used. This exemplifies the transfer pricing problem, in that:

1. divisional managers may hold legitimately different opinions of the future market price of an intermediate good or service;
2. divisional managers have the authority to use alternative suppliers or purchasers without recourse to the corporate management;
3. divisional managers are not required to transmit information centrally before making the decision.
4. the externally available goods or services are equivalent to those available internally.

With the divisional managers holding different views of the future market price, it is possible that protracted internal negotiations will result in the internal trade not taking place. Dependent on the alternatives available to both divisions, this decision would not be in the corporate interests, because the contribution is positive (£100 − 25 − 35 = £40 per unit). However, if the external intermediate market is imperfectly competitive, there is the possibility that sales may be made at £60 and purchases at £40, to the benefit of both divisions and the company. A system of transfer pricing which therefore allows managers to back their judgement is needed, but also one which ultimately does not harm the divisions, should the internal trade occur.

The fair and neutral approach emphasises the procedure by which the transfer price should be determined. Coinciding with the budget-setting time period, the divisional managers should meet to discuss the possibility of the internal trade taking place. The information given in Figure 2.4 should be available. The fair and neutral approach indicates how the transfer price will be set.

- Product cost = standard variable or out-of-pocket cost of supplying division
- Period cost = actual contribution earned by selling division in the budget period from the external sale of the intermediate good or service discovered ex post.

At this budget-setting stage, the total transfer price per unit will not be fixed, but the way in which it will be calculated is known.

For Indistinct plc, the transfer price may be in the range £40–60.

EXAMPLE 2.3

Calculating the transfer price

	Supplying division's estimate proves accurate		*Purchasing division's estimate proves accurate*
Product cost	£25 per unit		£25 per unit
Period cost			
(£60 – 25)	<u>35</u> per unit	(£40 – 25)	<u>15</u> per unit
Transfer price	<u>£60</u>		<u>£40</u>

Whatever actually transpires in the external market will be reflected in the period cost when the budget period ends and the divisional managers will be no worse off than competitors who have purchased from the selling division.

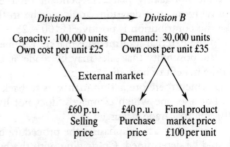

Division A ———————→ Division B

Capacity: 100,000 units   Demand: 30,000 units
Own cost per unit £25   Own cost per unit £35

External market

£60 p.u.   £40 p.u.   Final product
Selling   Purchase   market price
price   price   £100 per unit

FIGURE 2.4 Indistinct plc – revisited

The divisional managers may still prefer to rely on their estimates of the future external market price and agree not to trade. In order to provide an incentive for the managers to seriously consider the internal trade, especially when operating at below full capacity, an imputed lost contribution charge can be placed on the supplying division. This represents the lost contribution to the firm of the purchasing division using the external market when the supplying division could provide the good or service. This lost contribution charge can be transformed into a maximum discounted transfer price which will leave the selling division no better or worse off, whether the internal trade occurs or does not occur. However, the purpose of the maximum discount is not to set the transfer price, but to extend the range of potential transfer price values in order that negotiations can take place in a constructive manner. The information associated with Indistinct plc helps to illustrate these points.

Maximum discounted transfer price:

$$(1 - d_{tj})M_s = 2S_t - M_b$$

where:

$(1 - d_{tj})$ is the discount;
M_s is the price the selling division manager estimates will apply in the future in the external market;
S_t is the standard variable or out-of-pocket costs for the supplying division;
M_b is the price the buying division manager estimates will apply in the future in the external market.

For Indistinct plc:

$$(1 - d_{tj})60 = 2(25) - 40$$
$$d_{tj} = 83.3\% \text{ maximum}$$

Minimum transfer price = £10 per unit

EXAMPLE 2.4

Divisional performance reports

(a) No internal trade:	Division A £		Division B £
Sales (70,000 units at £60)	4,200K	Sales (30,000 units at £100)	3,000K
Own costs (70,000 units at £25)	1,750K	Own costs (30,000 units at £35)	
	2,450		1,050K
		External purchases (30K at £40)	1,200K

Lost contribution
charge
(100,000 – 70,000)

(£40 – 25)	450K	
Contribution	£2,000K	750K

(b) With internal trade:

	Division A £		Division B £
Sales (70,000 units at £60)	4,200K	Sales (30,000 units at £100)	3,000K
(30,000 units at £10)	300K		
	4,500	Own costs (30,000 units at £35)	1,050K
		Transfer price	
Own costs (100,000 units at £25)	2,500K	(30,000 units at £10)	300K
	£2,000K		£1,650K
Contribution			

The impact of these calculations on the manager of Division A should reinforce the extended range of negotiation to between £10 to £60 per unit. Given the uncertainty concerning the future market price, let us assume that the internal trade is agreed for 30,000 units. At the end of the period, it is discovered that the average revenue obtained by the selling division in the external market is £48 per unit. The period cost then becomes £23 per unit (£48 – 25 per unit). With the product cost, this amounts to a transfer price of £48 per unit.

Neither divisional manager is disadvantaged with respect to external competitors by this price. The period cost is verifiable, the actual revenue having been earned in this period but discovered after the event. The period cost is influenced by the selling division's marketing and sales effectiveness, and nothing else. This can be upheld if the level of external sales is regarded as significant relative to the total available capacity. Should the proportion of external market involvement decline, corporate management should question the merits of the separate profit-responsible status of the selling division. Any combination of inter-divisional trade is permitted – not merely zero or 30,000 units in this example – and improvements in profit performance are possible – for example, if Division A can sell extra output at above £48 per unit, or if Division B can purchase at below £48 per unit. The flexibility allows each divisional manager to follow their judgement, but the implications of operating at below full capacity or purchasing at above the ultimate transfer price will be apparent. For these reasons, it is suggested that this approach seeks to maintain divisional autonomy but allows the consequences of operating decisions of the make-or-buy type to be clearly seen.

ACTIVITY-BASED TRANSFER PRICES

The earlier summary of full cost transfer pricing suggested that ABC might prove useful in valuing inter-divisional trade, especially if a longer-term perspective is taken. In the long-run, a significant proportion of costs are variable and this should be recognised when tracing costs to products. The cost drivers of certain activities require identification and form the basis of product cost determination. To date, the use of ABC to charge out central services like computer services and research and development have been suggested, but there are isolated examples of potential use in banks (Sharma, 1992) and transportation (Bremser and Licata, 1991).

TARGET COSTING

The emergence of integrated and flexible manufacturing has prompted the development of a search for transfer price bases which recognise the importance of the product life cycle (Senn, 1990). Considerations of the market for the finished product determine design and development costs, which in turn determine the intermediate service and product costs at stages of the production cycle. Target costs are established for the final product in advance, and intermediate product and service values are derived from these. Hence, the transfer price is a function of the competitive selling price of the final product, development costs which are to be sustained, and the product life cycle (Kaplan and Atkinson, 1989). This is a similar approach to the resale price method which awards a level of return or profit to supplying divisions on the basis of the final product selling price. However, the inclusion of the product life cycle adds a further dimension to target costing.

Both ABC and target costing contain underlying philosophies which are likely to influence the universal applicability of the resulting transfer pricing approaches. At this stage, it is only possible to recognise their potential usefulness in avoiding re-centralisation of information.

SYNOPSIS

Consideration of a wide range of transfer pricing bases suggests that all are flawed to some extent if:

1. divisional autonomy over the make-or-buy decision is to be maintained;
2. freedom to use external markets is to be sustained; and
3. the centralisation of information flows is to be avoided.

This applies to the marginal cost, market oriented and shadow price approaches. Other approaches such as the pragmatic–analytical full cost and negotiation, fair and neutral approach, ABC and target costing require further consideration. However, it is apparent that even these approaches are unlikely to provide a universal solution. They, and the previous bases, may be capable of working effectively in particular situations. If, for example, there is no need to create profit centres, variable cost based transfer prices may ensure "optimal" solutions.

This suggests that an analysis on a broader plane is required in order to evaluate different transfer pricing approaches and bases. In particular, that transfer pricing is recognised within organisational contexts. In later chapters, the attempts to build explanatory frameworks of transfer pricing systems are examined with the need for divisional management participation and negotiation explicitly recognised. It is only at this level that it is likely that the contribution of certain transfer price bases to effective management control can be evaluated. Before this, however, the international dimension requires investigation.

QUESTIONS

1. Outline the limitations of the accountant's general rule to determining transfer prices.
2. Division Blanche has the opportunity to obtain a contract which would provide Hidgets at a price of £10 per unit. Incremental production costs are £1 per unit. Alternatively, a sister division, Noir, would use the Hidgets to make a final product which sells to external third parties at £25 per unit. Noir incurs incremental processing and marketing costs of £15 per unit. Blanche has set a transfer price of £10 per unit.

   Should the internal trade take place?

   What transfer price should be used?
3. The Burnbrae Company consists of two divisions which trade extensively with each other. The relevant revenue and cost functions for the core product are given below.

Average revenue, transferee division   £810 – 8Q
Average cost, transferee division   £10Q
Average cost, transferor division   £250 + 5Q

Q is the quantity to be traded internally

Determine the optimal transfer price, output level, corporate and separate divisional profits.

What might the transferee divisional manager contemplate under this system of transfer pricing?

4. "Optimal decision-making can be obtained in transfer pricing, but only at the cost of constraining decentralisation." Discuss.

5. In the Incorrigible plc example, the cost estimates have changed for Division L. These are as follows:

Sales / output (units)	Total cost
1,000	£2,000
2,000	£2,600
3,000	£3,300
4,000	£4,100
5,000	£5,000
6,000	£6,000

All other cost and revenue data remains as described originally.

Find the optimal output level, transfer price, corporate and separate divisional profits. Identify clearly the limitations of applying the economists approach.

6. "Applying a market-oriented approach to transfer pricing can be regarded as low cost in terms of information provision." By means of Gould's analysis, evaluate this statement.

7. "The transfer pricing basis is contingent on three variables which influence the degree of decentralisation." Critically evaluate this statement.

3

Transfer Pricing in Practice

INTRODUCTION

Transfer pricing has always been a practical issue, even though more academic effort has been expended on building theoretical models than on studying and explaining practice, since the problem started attracting serious attention. Over sixty years ago, Camman (1929, p. 37) stated that "the question is not an academic one. On the contrary it is very practical and is of increasing importance as the result of industrial expansion and combination". Camman's assertion is empirically verifiable as the trend towards expansion gained momentum, especially after the Second World War. The birth of the large multi-divisional (or M-form) company, first in the USA (Chandler, 1962 and 1977; Williamson, 1975, 1985 and 1986) and then its spread across Western Europe and Japan (Channon, 1973 and 1982; Goold and Campbell, 1987; and Pascale and Athos, 1982) resulted in what became known as "managerial capitalism" (Chandler and Daems, 1980). The advent of the multi-divisional or M-form company and the profit centre structure made transfer pricing the norm rather than the exception.

Recent archival evidence shows that some form of transfer pricing existed even in the last two centuries in the United Kingdom, in cotton mills (Stone, 1973), the textile industry (Mepham, 1983 and 1988); and in Scottish ironworks (Fleischman and Parker, 1990). Modern transfer pricing is identified as a by-product of decentralisation of the large company and the advent of the divisionalised company in the USA in the early 1920s (Hirshleifer, 1964; Johnson, 1978; Kaplan, 1984; Ansoff and McDonell, 1990; Eccles, 1985a; and Johnson and Kaplan, 1987). Pascale and Athos (1982) also provide evidence on early Japanese transfer pricing practice at the Matsushita company; Forrester (1977) and Drumm (1983) refer to the works of Professor Schmalembach on early transfer pricing theory and practice in Germany.

This chapter reviews, summarises and compares major empirical studies on domestic and multinational transfer pricing in different countries. Over fifty studies have now been published, most of these in the 1970s and 1980s. The earliest study known was published by the National Association of Accountants (NAA) in the USA in 1956 and coincided with the publication of four theoretical articles, by Cook (1955), Dean (1955); Stone (1956) and, most importantly, Hirshleifer's (1956) microeconomic approach. Although in most empirical studies the data were obtained via mail questionnaires – a data collection method not always flawless – it remains the case that the published surveys are virtually the only available insights on company practice. Annual published financial statements do not normally disclose information on internal trade and transfer pricing policies, although in some countries tighter regulations are being introduced to control transfer pricing activities, especially across national frontiers (Halperin and Srinidhi, 1991; Cole, 1991; Kee and Jeong, 1991; and Tang, 1992).

A CHRONOLOGY OF TRANSFER PRICING PRACTICE

A chronological grouping of surveys is adequate here in order to assess the evolution of the transfer pricing issue in line with the evolution of challenges to the business firm as well as the evolution of management systems in general and management accounting thought in particular. Transfer pricing has traditionally been treated as a cost–revenue problem and, to some extent, as a management accounting problem, but very seldom were the organisational, managerial or strategic dimensions of this thorny issue studied systematically. A succinct account of the evolution of the modern business firm and the development of management systems is provided by Chandler (1977), Chandler and Daems (1980), and Ansoff and McDonnell (1990). A similar account on the evolution of cost and management accounting is provided by Kaplan (1984), Johnson and Kaplan (1987) and Ezzamel and Hart (1987). Their path-finding syntheses indicate that, for the last sixty years or so, there has not been much development in management accounting procedures. Hence Kaplan (1984, p. 403) contended that existing transfer pricing practice "would be indistinguishable from that of thirty years ago, when the transfer pricing problem first attracted the attention of academics". The present review substantiates Kaplan's assertion, as most studies reported similar transfer pricing patterns, without, however, trying to place them in their organisational context.

Transfer pricing in the 1950s

As stated earlier, the first published survey, and the only one in the 1950s, was the NAA's (1956) study. This indicates that little is known about company practices in the first five decades of this century, except for a few hints about the existence of TPS early this century in the USA (Johnson, 1978; and Kaplan, 1984) and in Japan (Pascale and Athos, 1982) and Germany (Forrester, 1977; and Drumm, 1983). In fact the chronological review of the literature shows that empirical research became of concern after the publication of the first important theoretical prescriptions by Cook (1955), Dean (1955) and Hirshleifer (1956). This is important, because it is from the 1950s onwards, i.e. after the Second World War, that a major escalation of environmental turbulence in terms of new technologies, competitive pressures and consumer attitudes, took place (Ansoff and McDonell, 1990). It was also during the 1950s that the emphasis shifted from cost accounting – or the determination of product costs for financial reporting requirements – to management accounting, which stresses the decision-relevance of cost information (Kaplan and Atkinson, 1989; Shank and Govindarajan, 1989; and Drury, 1992).*

The results of the NAA (1956) study revealed that the majority of the forty participating companies used transfer prices which exceeded cost, adding a profit mark-up to yield a desired rate of return on sales or investment. Control of return on invested capital was a major objective of the transfer pricing system (TPS). The return on investment (ROI) performance criterion was pioneered by American companies in the early 1920s and is still a widely used performance measure of organisational units. The NAA survey reported that, in most cases, divisions were set up as quasi-profit centres, whereby divisional competition was sought as an incentive to profit consciousness. In most cases, however, transfer prices were centrally determined and divisional performance was judged in terms of overall corporate profits.

Transfer pricing in the 1960s

During the 1960s there was a noticeable increase in the trend toward decentralisation and the profit-centre structure. More information on

---

*This shift of emphasis was simultaneous in the UK as the interest in management accounting developed rapidly following the visit of the Anglo-American Council on Productivity team on Management Accounting to the USA in 1950 (Sizer, 1979; Ezzamel and Hart, 1987; and Armstrong and Jones, 1992).

transfer pricing practice became available with the publication of eight studies; six in the USA and two in the UK (Table 3.1). The most important of these was Solomons' (1965) comprehensive study of divisional performance measurement. The period of the 1960s is similar to the 1950s, as no particular changes took place, with the notable exception that quantitative analysis became a pivotal element in management accounting research (Kaplan, 1984; Drury, 1992). Transfer pricing was no exception to this mathematical inclination. The transfer pricing literature of the 1960s is replete with mathematical programming models for determining optimum transfer prices that would achieve efficient allocation of resources under capacity constraints.* However, the review and discussion of company practice in later sections in this chapter shows that, because of their complexity, mathematical models had few managerial implications, thus implying the existence of a gulf between theoretical prescriptions and company practice.

The publication of the first two studies on British transfer pricing practice by Livesey (1967) and Piper (1969) indicates that transfer pricing systems were operational in the modern British company not later than the early 1960s, and reflects the emulation of many of the features of the American M-form company after the Second World War. Surveys of British company transfer pricing practice have since gained in momentum.

Transfer pricing in the 1970s

The period of the 1970s is mainly marked by the emergence of the information-economics approach to management accounting which focuses on the economic nature of information, the demand for information, its value and its financial and non-financial costs (Kaplan, 1984; Ezzamel and Hart, 1987; Kaplan and Atkinson, 1989; and Drury, 1992) as well as an interest in the concept of corporate strategy (Armstrong and Jones, 1992). During this period there was a particular boom in both the theoretical and empirical literature on transfer pricing, a total of twenty studies being published (Table 3.2). As in the previous decade, there was no practical enthusiasm for the many mathematical prescriptions that appeared in academic papers. However, one major difference from the previous decade is the importance paid by American researchers to cross-border transfers or multinational transfer pricing, pointing to the prominence of the American multinational company in the early 1970s, the period of the oil boom.

A common feature that recurred in the studies was their focus on the impact of differential taxes and tariffs on cross-border transfer pricing.

---

*For a comprehensive review of the literature, see Thomas (1980) and Grabski (1985).

TABLE 3.1 Surveys of transfer pricing practice in the 1960s

Year and country	Authors	Issues covered and / or results
1964: USA	Winston	* availability of competitive market prices; * cost-based transfer prices plus mark-ups; * arbitrariness of mark-ups; * centralised pricing and sourcing decisions; * transfer pricing disputes and central intervention; * performance evaluation and the effect of uncontrollable factors on conflict.
1965: USA	Solomons; B.I.C.[a][M]	* objectives of TPS (performance evaluation and goal congruence); * widespread use of market-based transfer prices; * no single best transfer pricing method; * preference for single formula pricing; * predominance of production cost plus mark-up.
1967: USA, UK	NICB[b]; Livesey	* widespread use of market-based prices and multiple prices; * cost-based plus profit mark-up; * freedom of sourcing; * pricing and sourcing decisions limited; * predominance of full cost transfer pricing but arbitrary mark-up added; * incompatibility among common TPS objectives.
1968: USA	Mautz	* variety of transfer prices; * market- and cost-based prices equally used.
1969; UK, USA	Piper; Shulman[M]	* predominance of (negotiated) market-based transfer prices; * divisional autonomy and competition encouraged; * congruence of divisional and company goals; * environmental variables not important; * cost-oriented transfer prices; * centrally imposed prices cause disproportionate sharing of income.

Notes: [a]BIC = Business International Corporation;
[b]NICB = National Industrial Conference Board;
[M] = focus on multinational transfer pricing.

TABLE 3.2 Surveys of transfer pricing practice in the 1970s

Year and country	Authors	Issues covered and/or results
1970: USA	Greene/Duerr[M]	* influence of tax and customs factors; * cost plus prices or negotiated market prices; * TPS related to profit attainment in subsidiary.
1971: USA	Bursk et al.[M]	* cost plus and arm's-length transfer prices, but centrally imposed TPS in 50% of cases; * profit performance evaluation and profit optimisation objective of TPS; * no single best solution to transfer pricing; * suggests two-part tariff formula.
1971: UK, Sweden	Rook; Arvidsson	* multiple transfer prices, and * some central control over transfer pricing; * multiple transfer prices; * predominance of market prices; * close control by centre on external sourcing and price determination.
1972: UK, Germany	Arpan;[M] MBS;[a] Drumm	* popularity of market-oriented pricing; * centrally fixed prices in non-American firms; * national differences in pricing guidelines; * constrained sourcing and pricing policies; * divisional (profit) performance objective of TPS; * full cost plus mark-up prices.
1973: UK	Channon; Tomkins UK	* centrally imposed TPS when transfers significant; * (negotiated) market-based prices when transfers not significant; * profit-based performance evaluation; * multiple transfer prices.
1974: USA	Larson	* restricted pricing and sourcing decisions; * little use of available market prices.
1975: UK, USA, Canada	Granick	* impact of national differences on TPS; * variety of transfer pricing practices.
1977: UK	Emmanuel	* variety of transfer pricing bases; * divisional performance objective of TPS; * dysfunctional aspects of market-based pricing; * sourcing decision restricted.

TABLE 3.2 Continued

Year and country	Authors	Issues covered and/or results
1978: UK, USA	Finnie; Wu & Sharp; Vancil	* profit objective of TPS; * considerable diversity of practice; * central control over most decisions; * firm size and diversification vs. amount of transfers; * widespread cost plus mark-up transfer prices; * importance of organisational mode on TPS; * domestic vs. multinational transfer pricing; * prevalence of negotiation or settling disputes.
1979: USA, Japan, Canada, Australia	Lambert; Tang; Kim & Miller;[M] Drury & Bates; Chenhall	* multiple transfer pricing schemes; * predominance of market prices; * high levels of divisional autonomy; * multiple profit indexes of performance; * transfer pricing of EDP[b] services; * predominance of full cost charge-back systems; * internal conflict; * no panacean transfer pricing method; * TPS in developing and developed countries; * income tax liabilities not an important factor; * impact of profit repatriation restrictions; exchange controls, and joint venture constraints; * Market and cost-oriented prices for domestic operations; * less cost-oriented multinational transfer prices.

Notes: [a]MBS = Manchester Business School;
[b]EDP = electronic data processing;
[M] = focus on multinational transfer pricing.

Global tax minimisation is a usual objective of the transfer pricing system in multinational companies. Another distinguishing feature is cross-cultural and comparative research. Arpan (1972) investigated the effects of cultural differences on internal pricing practices of sixty non-US multinationals, while Granick (1975) studied the relationship between and impact of national differences in Britain, France and the USA on transfer pricing policies. Wu and Sharp (1979) examined and contrasted the domestic and multinational transfer pricing practices of large American multinational companies. Milburn's (1978) study reported on the multinational practices of US and Canadian companies; whereas Tang (1979) compared domestic and multinational practices of US and Japanese companies.

The above studies tried to identify transfer pricing determinants in different cultures and reported on some cultural influences on the determination of internal pricing practices. These studies coincided with the awareness that tax authorities like the Inland Revenue in the UK and the Internal Revenue Service in the USA developed methods to circumvent fraudulent transfer pricing activities. A classical case of profit misrepresentation and tax evasion through transfer price manipulation is that of the Swiss pharmaceutical firm, Hoffman-LaRoche, which was fined £1.85 billions in back taxes by the British government (Choi and Mueller, 1978; Reekie and Weber, 1979; and Stopford *et al.*, 1980). This particular issue will be developed further in the next three chapters.

It is also worth noting that British transfer pricing attracted more academic attention during the 1970s, with the publication of the results of the first two Ph.D research projects on the subject by Channon (1973) and Emmanuel (1977). Channon's study was reminiscent of Chandler's (1962) *Strategy and Structure* study of American companies, while Emmanuel's project investigated the factors that influenced transfer pricing choice. No particular study reflected the short-lived information-economics approach that emerged in the mid-1970s and which was subsequently supplanted by the principal–agent theory approach.*

Transfer pricing in the 1980s and 1990s

The 1980s and 1990s constitute an interesting period for the study of transfer pricing, because of the challenges brought about by new manufacturing technology like computer aided design (CAD), computer integrated manufacturing (CIM) and flexible manufacturing systems (FMS). This has opened a new chapter in the history of management accounting, as the emphasis has now shifted to strategic cost analysis with activity-based costing (ABC) and cost drivers; just in time (JIT) and zero stock levels; target costing; and total quality control and management (TQC/TQM) among the fashionable vocabulary.

The period since 1980 has seen a surge in research on transfer pricing practice, but it is only in the last few years that there have been real changes in research emphasis (Table 3.3). Once again there were some mathematical models proposed, but with no evidence as to their usefulness in practice or, as Baiman (1982) and Scapens *et al.* (1983) put it, mathematical elegance had taken precedence over practical usefulness. There was also a noticeable increase in the comparative and hybrid type of studies started in the 1970s. It remains the case, however, that there

---

*See Chapter 6 for a principal–agent approach to transfer pricing.

TABLE 3.3 Surveys of transfer pricing practice in the 1980s and 1990s

Year and country	*Authors*	*Issues covered and/or results*
1980: USA	Benke/Edwards; Burns; Bavishi/Wyman;	* predominance of market-based prices; * influence of market conditions, competition and subsidiary profitability on transfer pricing; * multiple transfer prices; two-part tariff transfer price; * income tax liabilities not important; * compliance with FASB 14.
1981: UK, Canada	Tang	* variety of transfer pricing methods; * wide use of market-based transfer prices; * profit-based TPS; * tax minimisation as major objective of TPS.
1982: UK, USA	Mostafa; Yunker; Scapens *et al.*; Czechowicz *et al.*	* single and multiple transfer pricing schemes and negotiation; * domestic market-based pricing vs. full cost multinational pricing; * importance of divisional autonomy, profits, foreign tax and tariff regulations; * small levels of internal trade; * central arbitration; * restricted external sourcing; * cost plus transfer prices and restricted divisional autonomy in US firms; * government regulations, raw material and labour costs as major price determinants; * (negotiated) market-based prices in non-US firms.
1983: India, Yugoslavia	Govindarajan & Ramamurthy; Sacks	* predominance of market-based and actual cost prices; * less autonomy to sell externally than to source externally; * importance of self management and worker participation; * market-based transfer prices; * performance-related pay.
1984: UK, USA	Whiting & Gee; Price Waterhouse	* method vs. process; * predominance of (negotiated) market prices; * performance evaluation objective of TPS; * importance of divisional autonomy; * no inter-divisional conflict; * no centrally imposed transfer prices.
1985: USA	Solomon & Tsay; Eccles	* EDP cost-based charge-back systems; * importance of goal congruence and performance evaluation; * necessity of multi-disciplinary approach; * importance of vertical integration, diversification, and administrative process; * different TPS for different situations.

TABLE 3.3 Continued

Year and country	Authors	Issues covered and/or results
1986: USA	Hoshower & Mandel	* testing of Eccles' (1985) theoretical framework; * market and cost-based transfer prices; * minimum central intervention.
1987: USA, Canada	Abdullah; Atkinson	* minimum use of TPS for international transfer of funds; * priority to tax considerations in TPS; * cost allocation vs. transfer pricing; * profit performance objective of TPS; * cost analysis objective of TPS; * market and cost-based transfer prices.
1990: UK, USA	Al-Eryani et al.; Borkowski; Mehafdi;	* US TPS in both developed and developing countries; * predominance of non-market-based transfer prices; * multiple transfer prices; * importance of tax and custom regulations and financial reporting considerations; * influence of environmental and organisational factors on transfer price choice; * negotiation and conflict; * divisional vs. company-based performance measures and conflict; * contingency theory and agency theory; * degree of decentralisation; degree of typical internal trade; locus of transfer pricing and sourcing decisions; * TPS role in the management control process; * restricted sourcing, high internal trade and mandated transfer prices; * insignificant internal trade and (negotiated) market transfer prices; * impact of TPS on divisional performance and conflict; * conflict and APM.
1991: France	Bafcop et al.	* Dominance of centrally fixed cost-based prices; * external sourcing highly restricted; * negligible negotiation; * financially driven divisional rewards but performance measurement not a TPS objective.
1992: USA	Tang	* New regulations on multinational transfer pricing; * variety of transfer pricing methods; * profit-driven TPS; * importance of the tax factor.

were more studies on American company practice than in any other single country. This pattern applies to research in the three preceding decades, thus showing the precedence of the American research effort on the complex issue of transfer pricing.

The only empirical evidence available so far on company practice in the 1990s is the recent study by Tang (1992), but there is nothing particularly unusual from the results of Tang's study. The other three studies included in Table 3.3 (Al-Eryani, Alam and Alchter, 1990; Borkowski, 1990; and Mehafdi, 1990) report in fact on company practice in the later years of the 1980s. In a recent article, Spicer (1992) refers to a working paper based on a case study by Spicer and Colbert (1992) which tries to establish the link between ABC systems and the TPS, without, however, giving any detail or results. Thus the scarcity of information on company practice in the present decade implies that we still do not know the impact of advanced manufacturing technology on TPS design, and the future of transfer pricing under ABC, JIT and target costing.

The idea of the flexible firm and focused factory and the decentralisation of decisions to factory and plant levels aim at achieving speedy and best quality production. The JIT philosophy puts the customer first in the list of priorities, while ABC and target costing are innovative techniques to synchronise better cost management with technological excellence. What is the role of the TPS under these new organisational and managerial circumstances? For instance, what is a full cost transfer price under ABC, knowing that both the definition and classification of costs have changed? In other words, if internal trade is part and parcel of the business of a company with advanced technology, what are the criteria for cost driver definition and selection to yield optimum transfer prices?

These and other questions lend themselves to worthwhile research, but for the present, we can only hypothesise that intra-company interdependence will possibly be dramatically reduced with new factory layouts, FMS, JIT purchasing and production, and the consequent scaling-down of centralised service departments. Alternatively one may speculate that transfer pricing might play a more prominent role under the new circumstances. Hence the opportunity to re-examine the ambiguous issue of transfer pricing from a completely different perspective is available. In fact we still do not even know enough about, nor do we fully understand, existing transfer pricing practices. Emmanuel (1977), Vancil (1978) and Govindarajan and Ramamurthy (1983) concluded their respective studies by stating their inability to explain the reasons why the companies they studied used particular methods or bases for pricing internal transactions.

The following sections will try to shed some light on observed company practices unveiled by the available studies grouped in Tables 3.1 to 3.8.

MAGNITUDE OF INTERNAL TRADE

Transfer pricing exists because an internal market exists for the exchange of goods and services between segments or divisions of the same organisation. The internalisation of trade has long raised the question as to why some economic activities are organised within rather than among independent firms (Coase, 1937), or what drives the preference of hierarchies over markets (Williamson, 1975, 1985 and 1986). For Coase, the firm reduces transaction costs by internalising a number of market transactions, and thus the firm supersedes the market for the allocation of resources. Williamson suggests that the answer to the above question depends, among other things, on the volume and frequency of the internal transaction, i.e. its material significance.

Information on internal trade and transfer pricing is, however, difficult to obtain. For instance, Gray and Radebaugh (1984) found that none of the thirty-five multinational British companies they surveyed disclosed information on internal sales. Only a few of the studies reviewed in this chapter reported the amount of internal trade (Table 3.4). It may also be that researchers have been more interested in the pricing methods than in the underlying reasons for and consequences of internal trade. Nevertheless, the scanty information available shows that the majority of companies surveyed reported a volume of transfers of less than 20% (Table 3.4). Very few companies have amounts of transfers of more than

TABLE 3.4 Material significance of internal trade (measured as a percentage of total company sales)

Study (author and year)	Country	Number of companies with transfers	Percentage of companies with transfers of:		
			Less than 10%	10% to 25%	More than 25%
Rook (1971)	UK	193	>50%	34%	negligible
M.B.S. (1972)	UK	44	43%	32%	25%
Channon (1973)	UK	22	N/A	N/A	41%
Vancil (1978)	USA	249	N/A	27%	
Tang (1981)	UK Canada	272	>50%	N/A	>25%
Scapens et al. (1982)	USA UK	N/A	N/A	N/A	18% U.S 15% U.K
Mehafdi (1990)	UK	33	55%	21%	24%

30% or 40%. Moreover, few studies tried to find out the reasons for the degree of internal trade.

In a recent study of domestic transfer pricing practice in the UK, Mehafdi (1990) found that the volume of internal trade varied from below 5% of total annual sales to 90%, in the thirty-three participating companies. No apparent association could be discerned between company size and the extent of internal trade. However, the high volumes of transfers observed in eight companies were found to be related to vertical integration (an aluminium company with 80% transfers); technological sensitivity (four electrical and electronics companies with 40% transfers); and speciality products with no intermediate markets (a tobacco company with 90% transfers, and two chemical/pharmaceuticals companies with 40% and 50% transfers). This finding supports the transaction costs theory of governance structure, which states that it is better to internalise frequent transactions which involve high asset specificity and uncertainty (Williamson, 1985).

The internalisation of these transactions also has a strategic dimension, or what Radner (1985) and Reve (1990) refer to as the "strategic core". The strategic core is defined as the set of highly specific assets which enable the company to attain its strategic objectives. Asset specificity includes technological and know-how advantages, and investments specific to certain transactions. For example, the pharmaceuticals company with 50% transfers in Mehafdi's (1990) sample mainly thrives on its R & D programmes to develop new medicines. This requires high levels of investments in specific assets, hence a strategy of centrally controlled internal trade to protect technological advantage. The importance of the strategic core also applies to the remaining seven companies with high volumes of internal trade in Mehafdi's sample.

THE INTERPLAY BETWEEN THE TPS AND PERFORMANCE EVALUATION

The managerial ambiguity inherent in the decentralised firm (Vancil, 1978) reflects itself best in the objectives traditionally assigned to the transfer pricing mechanism. The TPS is usually expected to satisfy simultaneously an array of conflicting objectives, which include divisional autonomy, managerial motivation and entrepreneurship, divisional performance evaluation, tax minimisation, profit maximisation and resource allocation. The incompatibility among these objectives becomes particularly manifest when divisional performance is not cocooned from the effects of the TPS.

If transfer pricing and cost allocation have been described as "incorrigible twins" (Emmanuel, Otley and Merchant, 1990), the interplay between transfer pricing and performance evaluation is even more para-doxical, especially when the internal transaction is material and the TPS is centrally administered. The obvious reason for the paradox is that divisional profit performance evaluation is usually a fundamental objective of the TPS. Profit centres are supposed to be autonomous entities with clear divisional demarcation lines, but the existence of internal trade and the TPS obscures divisional boundaries and gives rise to all sorts of disagreements between the parties to the internal transaction. Companies resort to negotiation or arbitration to resolve conflicts but this sometimes leads to an aggravation of hostilities when the interplay between the TPS and divisional performance is not handled properly. The important issue of transfer pricing conflict is discussed in detail in Chapter 7.

The interplay between the TPS and performance evaluation is a recurring theme in Tables 3.1–3.3 and is common to both domestic and multinational operations. The main issue is whether to judge divisional performance on divisional or corporate results – that is, whether or not to include the effect of the TPS on performance in segmental reporting. The studies by Whinston (1964), Lambert (1979), Eccles (1985a), Bor-kowski (1990) and Mehafdi (1990) report on the cause–effect relationship between the performance evaluation objective of the TPS and internal conflict in the companies they surveyed. Their results show that transfer pricing is not really a mere technical problem which can easily be solved by a clever cost formula, but is rather an issue of strategy, structure, technology and human behaviour, the combination of which requires dynamic TPS and flexible performance measurement, evaluation and reward systems (PMERS). These are agency issues, but since agency theory does not provide a set of parameters to measure agency costs and benefits, only speculative judgements may be inferred from the available observations of practice. Agency-based theoretical models of cost allocations and transfer pricing are reviewed in Chapter 6. We see this as a potential area for positive research to enrich agency theory and the development of efficient management accounting systems.

Transfer pricing practices

The results of surveys of company practice over the last thirty years or so show that transfer pricing practice is marked by great diversity. The selected data summarised in Tables 3.5 to 3.7 below reflect the diversity of both domestic and multinational practice. There are many reasons why it is virtually impossible to discern a consistent pattern of internal pricing, whether over time or across countries. The companies studied vary in sample size and industrial mix and, therefore, a perfect comparative analysis of their pricing practices is not feasible. Secondly, there is a noticeable lack of focus in many of the studies, as they do not report

TABLE 3.5 British domestic transfer pricing practices

Companies and transfer pricing:	Author and year						
	Rook 1971	MBS 1972	Tomkins 1973	Emmanuel 1977	Tang 1981	Mostafa 1982	Mehafdi 1990
Participating:	193	44	51	92	80	46	35
Less non-usable:	–	–	7	–	17	5	2
Usable replies:	193	44	44	92	63	41	33
	%	%	%	%	%	%	%
Pricing basis:							
Cost-based	**46.1[a]**	**63.6**	**45.4**	**35.9**	**68.3**	**34.1**	**36.3**
Variable cost:							
at standard		*6.8*	*6.8*	*2.2*			
at actual				*2.2*	*3.2*		
Variable cost plus			*13.6*		*3.2*	*7.3*	*6.1*
Full cost:	*46.1*	*45.5*		*17.4*	*33.3*	*9.7*	*15.1*
at standard	*28.5*	*25.0*	*6.8*	*13.0*	*19.0*	*2.4*	
at actual	*17.6*	*20.5*		*4.4*	*14.3*	*7.3*	
Full cost plus		*11.4*	*18.2*	*16.3*	*25.4*	*17.1*	*15.1*
Market-based	**53.9[a]**	**36.4**	**70.4**	**44.6**	**36.5**	**46.3**	**45.5**
current price	*22.3*	*25.0*	*50.0*	*27.2*	*31.7*	*29.2*	*27.3*
adjusted	*31.6*	*11.4*	*20.4*	*17.4*	*4.8*	*17.1*	*18.2*
Negotiated[b]	**16.6**	**16.6**	**31.8**	**19.6**	**33.3**	**26.8**	**42.4**
Other[b]			**4.5**		**9.5**	**7.3**	

Notes: [a] percentage of usable sample with cost- or market-based transfer prices. Total percentage may exceed 100%, as some companies use more than one transfer pricing basis.

TABLE 3.6 Domestic transfer pricing practices in other countries

Country, author and year

Companies and transfer pricing:	Vancil 1978	USA Tang 1979	Tang 1992	Germany Drumm 1972	Japan Tang 1979	Canada Tang 1981	Australia Chenhall 1979	France Bäfcop et al. 1991
Participating:	291	145	143	24	102	192	173	62
Less non-usable:	52	12	11	–	28	29	69	16
Usable replies:	239	133	132	24	74	163	104	46
Pricing basis:	%	%	%	%	%	%	%	%
*Cost-based:	**46.8[a]**	**85.0**	**76.5**	**41.6**	**74.3**	**62.0**	**51.9**	**70.0**
Variable cost:	4.6	5.3	6.1	8.3			5.8	15.1
at standard	3.0					1.8		
at actual	1.6					4.3		
Variable cost plus		1.5	1.5		1.4	1.8		6.1
Full cost:	25.5	45.1	41.0	12.5	1.4		3.8	36.4
at standard	12.5	29.3	25.8		24.3	18.4	21.1	27.3
at actual	13.0	15.8	15.2		14.8	12.9		9.1
Full cost plus	16.7	33.1	28.0	20.8	32.4	22.7	21.1	12.1
*Market-based	**31.0[a]**	**51.9**	**55.3**	**45.8**	**54.0**	**50.3**	**53.8**	**9.1**
current price		37.6	42.4	4.2	28.4	38.0		3.0
adjusted		14.3	12.9	41.6	25.6	12.3		6.1
*Negotiated[b]	**22.2**	**31.6**	**28.0**	**12.5**	**31.1**	**27.6**	**10.6**	**12.1**
*Other[b]		**6.0**	**9.1**		**1.4**			**9.1**

Notes: [a]Percentage of usable sample with cost- or market-based transfer prices. Total percentage may exceed 100% as some companies use more than one transfer pricing basis.   [b]Includes both cost- and market-based transfer prices.

TABLE 3.7 Multinational transfer pricing practices

Companies and transfer prices:	USA		UK			Japan	Canada
	Wu and Sharp 1978	Tang 1979	Tang 1992	Tang 1981	Mostafa 1982	Tang 1979	Tang 1981
Participating:	209	145	143	80	132	102	192
Less non-usable:	–	12	53	17	86	26	29
Usable replies:	209	133	90	63	46	74	163
	%	%	%	%	%	%	%
Pricing basis:							
*Cost based	**36.4**[a]	**40.0**	**70.0**	**36.5**	**30.4**	**35.1**	**20.8**
Variable cost:		*0.8*	*2.2*			*1.3*	*1.8*
at standard							
at actual							
Variable cost plus		*1.5*		*3.2*	*4.3*	*1.3*	*1.8*
Full cost:	7.7	*9.0*	*18.9*	*7.9*	*6.5*		*4.3*
at standard		*4.5*	*12.2*	*3.2*		*4.1*	*2.5*
at actual		*4.5*	*6.7*	*4.7*		*4.1*	*1.8*
Full cost plus	28.7	28.6	46.7	25.4	19.6	28.4	12.9
*Market-based	**41.6**[a]	**31.0**	**66.7**	**38.1**	**17.4**	**31.1**	**24.5**
current price	25.4	18.0	45.6	27.0	13.0	19.0	17.8
adjusted	16.2	13.0	21.1	11.1	4.4	12.1	6.7
*Negotiated[b]	**24.9**	**12.0**	**22.2**	**30.1**	**15.2**	**19**	**17.2**
*Other[b]	**6.2**	**1.5**	**15.5**	**7.9**	**15.2**		**3.7**

Notes: [a]Percentage of usable sample with cost- or market-based transfer prices. Total percentage may exceed 100% as some companies use more than one transfer pricing basis.
[b]Includes both cost- and market-based transfer prices.

on typical transfer pricing practice but on general transfer pricing methods used. Most importantly, the strategic, organisational and behavioural dimensions of company practice are almost excluded by most of the studies, thus ignoring the context of the transfer pricing problem in the decentralised firm. Notwithstanding these shortcomings, useful conclusions can still be derived by making some insights into the variables and the themes covered by the different studies from both the domestic and multinational perspectives.

What is commonly observed in many of the cases is the use of multiple bases for determining transfer prices, the widespread use of value-added pricing (market-based and full cost plus mark-up) and negotiated pricing. The rules and regulations of negotiation are, however, seldom reported by the studies, although in a few cases (e.g. Lambert, 1979; Eccles, 1985a; Mehafdi, 1990; and Borkowski, 1990) the relationship between negotiation and other dimensions of transfer pricing is established, in particular the cause–effect relationship with conflict.

Domestic transfer pricing: variables studied and major results

Tables 3.5 and 3.6 summarise domestic transfer pricing practices reported by some of the studies over the last two decades in the UK, USA and other countries. Except for Vancil (1978), no statistically significant relationship between firm size and the extent of internal transfers was reported. The most common and recurring feature of all the studies is the comparison between cost-based and market-based transfer prices, though such comparison is not always conclusive. For instance, the use of cost-based pricing does not rule out the existence of market prices for the intermediate product, yet very few studies examined this issue. In general, the majority of companies use transfer prices which exceed cost. A profit mark-up is calculated to yield a desired rate of return on sales or investment. The addition of a mark-up, usually determined arbitrarily, to full cost indicates that the transfers of goods are treated as market purchase and sale transactions, regardless of whether market prices are taken into account or not. However, the reasons for the predominance of a particular transfer pricing policy are seldom made explicit or even alluded to.

Some of the studies do, however, highlight the causal relationship between restrictions on using the external market and the extent of transfer pricing conflict (e.g. Larson, 1974; Lambert, 1979). In many cases, the freedom to trade with the external market was restricted and required approval from central management (e.g. Whinston, 1964). Similarly, many surveys reported that transfer prices were largely arbitrary and established by headquarters staff.

Multinational transfer pricing: variables studied and main results

The comparison between cost-based and market-based transfer prices is also a recurring issue in the studies of multinational transfer pricing. Again, as can be gleaned from the data in Table 3.7, this comparison is not particularly conclusive, though it is apparent from many studies that, similar to domestic transfer pricing, there is no perfect or universally optimal system of intra-corporate pricing in the multinational context. Corporate policies on international transfer pricing are generally found to be influenced by constant pressures from internal as well as exogenous factors, and this naturally requires variability and adaptability in the TPS. For instance, in designing their TPS, companies try to comply with the "arm's-length" principle required by tax authorities for multinational transfer pricing, while at the same time satisfying their own objectives and the regulations of the host country. The arm's-length rule is discussed in later chapters. In most cases, the use of a pricing policy, be it market-based or cost plus, is found to be primarily driven by the maximisation of consolidated profits and subsidiary performance evaluation. These are the key objectives usually attributed to the TPS in the multinational context. Bonuses for executives were found to be based directly on profit performance.

Some studies explain the difference between transfer pricing practices in terms of the degree of decentralisation. In highly decentralised multinationals, subsidiary managers are found to enjoy greater autonomy in establishing transfer prices, hence the use of market-based pricing; whereas cost-based pricing usually indicates centrally administered TPS.

In addition to the variables examined by domestic studies, surveys of transfer pricing practice across national frontiers pay special attention to a set of environmental factors such as anti-dumping legislation, exchange controls, currency fluctuations, profit repatriation, and tax and customs duty considerations. These factors are specific to overseas operations and are particularly pertinent to short-term financial objectives, hence the importance attached to them by multinationals in framing their transfer policies. As stated above, it is common to many of the studies to report that the key objectives of the TPS are the maximisation of consolidated profits and subsidiary performance evaluation. Thus, the existence of varying rates of taxation across national frontiers is in itself an obvious incentive for transfer price manipulation for the sake of maximising profits.

On the other hand, very few studies looked at the long-term and strategic dimensions of multinational transfer pricing, such as the level of competition, market conditions, unstable host governments, public relations and joint venture considerations with foreign partners. The predominance of the short-term determinants reflects the tight measures that host governments have adopted to prevent tax evasion through the manipulation of transfer pricing between the parent company and the subsidiaries operating in the host countries. This point is discussed in detail in Chapters 4 and 5.

SYNOPSIS

Transfer pricing practice is marked by great diversity, whether for domestic or international intra-corporate operations. The multiplicity of transfer pricing methods and the diversity of policies observed from the data summarised in the tables above all point to the fact that there is no universal or cure-all TPS. None the less, better insights into the complexities of this problem can be gained when the research methodology encompasses not only the technical aspects, but also the organisational and behavioural dimensions. Whether a company applies a market price, a cost price, or multiple pricing is not really the crux of the issue. A pricing formula can easily be derived and administered, but its behavioural and long-term consequences may be overlooked. Thus, what is more important is whether the TPS befits the strategic and structural circumstances of the particular company, and reflects the operational realities of the divisions involved in the internal trade.

QUESTIONS

1. Discuss the development of transfer pricing empirical research and comment on the assertions made in this chapter on the phases of management accounting thought.
2. Diagnose the methodological deficiencies of past surveys of transfer pricing practice, and propose ways of improvement.
3. Comment on the transfer pricing practices reported by the different studies using time, space and culture as parameters.
4. Discuss the key determinants of multinational transfer pricing policies from a corporate strategy perspective. How would these determinants change in the 1990s because of the drastic changes observed in the global market?
5. Using your analysis of the diverse company pricing practices, discuss the divergence between theoretical prescriptions and practice and evaluate the validity of existing transfer pricing theories.
6. Market-based and negotiated transfer prices are widely used in practice. If your company decides to use target costing, how would this affect transfer price setting and the negotiation process?

7. With the help of numerical examples, show how activity based costing and throughput accounting can contribute to the search for optimum transfer prices. You may refer to the analyses in the previous two chapters.
8. In your opinion, what is the future of transfer pricing in highly automated, flatter organisations with just-in-time systems?

4

Key Players and Conflicting Goals in Multinational Transfer Pricing

INTRODUCTION

MNE pricing practices associated with cross-border transfers of goods and services have more than once hit the headlines. "Standard's US deal runs into tax snag" (*Sunday Times*, 2 July, 1978), "Denmark's tax bombshell" (*Financial Times*, 7 February, 1978), "Revenue hits Glaxo on £8m profit" (*Accountancy Age*, 20 January, 1978), "Oil companies attacked on transfer pricing issue" (*Accountancy Age*, 27 April, 1979), "Butchering the revenue" (*Economist*, 11 October, 1980) are just a selection. Nor has the coverage dwindled over time. "Transfer pricing: the Revenue speaks" (*Certified Accountant*, January 1987), "Inland Revenue probes tax avoidance at Sony" (*Sunday Times*, 22 March, 1992) and "IRS investigates foreign companies for tax cheating" (*New York Times*, 18 February, 1990), "Apple Computer fights claim by IRS" (*New York Times*, 3 April 1993) testify to the persistence and international nature of the issue. And whilst compliance with tax regulations is an important aspect, it is not the only one. MNEs also appear to adopt international transfer prices which accord with tariff regulations, economic restrictions, governmental regulations and the political environment (Wu and Sharp, 1979). At a point in time, these constraints may not be mutually supportive. In addition, there are the roles international transfer prices may fulfil in promoting goal congruence, subsidiary performance evaluation, competitive advantage and currency stabilisation within the enterprise (Borkowski, 1992). In comparison with domestic transfer pricing, the complexity of the international situation is apparent. The scale of international trade conducted between subsidiaries of MNEs reveals that this is not a trivial problem.

In 1973, the United Nations reported that 30% of UK exports were intra-group by nature. It was stated that "these figures are based on sampling procedures and are therefore prone to error, but the errors are likely to be small in comparison to the magnitude of the base figures" (UN, 1978). More recently, Dunning and Pearce (1985) stated that intra-group trading in Europe accounted for 33% of all exports, with the percentage rising to in excess of 50% for certain industries, such as computers, pharmaceuticals and motor vehicles. The continual expansion of MNEs by means of international acquisitions meant that by 1990, foreign-owned assets in the USA, for example, had tripled during the 1980s to $1.8 trillion. However, the aggregate taxes paid had hardly changed, and of the 36,800 foreign-owned companies filing returns in 1986, more than half reported no taxable income (Pear, 1990). The US Treasury believed that $100 billion of taxes had been avoided by thirty-six multinationals, two-thirds of them Japanese, by manipulating transfer prices during the period 1980 to 1990.

A similar investigation in the UK revealed that British and foreign (non-Japanese) MNEs paid five times as much tax per pound of turnover as their Japanese counterparts. In 1988–9 and 1990–1, the Inland Revenue collected less than £40 million in profits tax from the 10 biggest Japanese firms in Britain. This represented only 0.6% of their combined UK turnover. It is in stark contrast with the £14 billion in profits tax which the largest ten British companies, including ICI, BAe and Unilever, paid during the same period (*Sunday Times*, 1992).

ACCOUNTING DISCLOSURE POLICIES

Precisely gauging the significance of intra-group transactions is not easy. Cases which do come to the courts have a tendency to be settled before the full details of transfer pricing are disclosed. Fiscal agencies can usually monitor out-bound transactions more easily than those that are in-bound, due to the availability of the books and records kept in English. MNE tax returns are not in the public domain and accounting disclosure policies concerning transfer pricing have yet to be harmonised. Nevertheless, the occasional report offers some insight.

Wheeler (1990) gave evidence to the House of Representatives Ways and Means Oversight Subcommittee, having gained access to the Statistics of Income Division of the Internal Revenue Service. His investigation revealed that for 1983–7 (see Table 4.1), the return on assets of all foreign-based US subsidiaries was less than 1%. Reported income for these subsidiaries fell over the period and was negative in 1986, yet dividends grew.

Evidence of tax avoidance can also be implied from examination of the 20-F annual report which all listed foreign corporations are required to produce for the Securities and Exchange Commission (SEC). A segment report giving separate disclosure of sales, operating profit and identifiable assets by major product line and by major geographic area can be provided. However, the SEC has waived this disclosure requirement for all listed foreign corporations filing Form 20-F (Wheeler, 1990). This placed US listed companies at a disadvantage, especially as FAS 14 (FASB, 1976) requires inter-segment sales to be shown and the basis of accounting for such transfers to be described.

Whilst having the waiver, Sony did not choose to exercise it in 1989 and provided the information contained in Table 4.2.

A straight-forward analysis indicates that foreign sales comprising 65.9% of the total, generated only 38.1% of the income before tax and only 28.8% of the current tax payments. In contrast, the Japanese government's proportion of tax seems excessive, given the level of reported sales.

A similar pattern emerged in the case of the British MNE, Beazer plc (Table 4.3). The segment report consistent with the 20-F filing reveals that in the years 1987 and 1988, 27% and 26% of total tangible fixed assets produced 56% and 69% respectively of corporate net income. A more positive relationship between the location of fixed assets and contribution to the enterprise's profit might have been expected.

The British MNE's filing did not give the tax liability by geographical segment. However, the disclosure is extensive, in comparison with the same company's disclosure when complying with UK requirements in operation at that time (Table 4.4).

The disparity is obvious. Under the different disclosure requirements in 1988, only the profit margin (or net income divided by sales) can be calculated under both UK and US presentations, and then for just 1987 and 1988. Even so, the figures are not perfectly consistent, suggesting that different generally accepted accounting principles are being employed.

Beazer's ROI and sales to investment ratios were only available under the US 20-F filing and suggest significant differences between the operations of the three geographical segments. Whether this was due to the MNEs transfer pricing policy is difficult to gauge.

Since the introduction of SSAP 25 in 1990, all British MNEs meeting certain size criteria have been required to disclose operating profit and net assets by geographical segment. This may be seen as a move towards

TABLE 4.1 Financial performance of foreign-owned US subsidiaries (dollar amounts in millions)

All foreign-owned US subsidiaries

Year	All returns	Total assets	Receipts	Income less deficit	Return on assets	Distributions	Distrib/receipts
1983	33,622	$530,334	$389,909	$1,849	0.35%	$4,327	1.110%
1984	37,401	$552,598	$459,162	$4,528	0.82%	$3,322	0.723%
1985	36,677	$655,696	$513,778	$2,978	0.45%	$3,529	0.687%
1986	36,778	$840,893	$542,695	($1,519)	−0.18%	$5,568	1.026%
1987	n/a	$959,400	$686,800	$5,600	0.58%	n/a	n/a

All foreign-owned US subsidiaries with income

Year	Returns	Total assets	Receipts	Net income	Return on assets	Distributions	Distrib/receipts
1983	13,648	n/a	$227,383	$12,448	n/a	$3,297	1.450%
1984	15,306	n/a	$295,319	$15,356	n/a	$2,599	0.880%
1985	15,882	n/a	$332,791	$14,500	n/a	$3,157	0.949%
1986	14,348	n/a	$335,840	$12,745	n/a	$2,904	0.865%
1987	n/a	n/a	n/a	n/a	n/a	n/a	n/a

All foreign-owned US subsidiaries with deficit

Year	Returns	Total assets	Receipts	Net deficit	Return on assets	Distributions	Distrib/receipts
1983	23,753	n/a	$162,526	($10,599)	n/a	$1,030	0.634%
1984	22,095	n/a	$163,843	($10,828)	n/a	$723	0.441%
1985	20,795	n/a	$180,987	($11,522)	n/a	$372	0.206%
1986	22,430	n/a	$206,855	($14,264)	n/a	$2,664	1.288%
1987	n/a	n/a	n/a	n/a	n/a	n/a	n/a

Source: Statistics of Income Division, IRS, reported by Wheeler (1990).

TABLE 4.2 Sony Corporation 20-F Segment Report 1989

Sales:		
Japan	$5,540,129	34.1%
US	4,441,500	27.3
Europe	3,771,530	23.2
All other	2,499,333	15.4
Total sales	$16,252,492	100.0%
Income before taxes:		
Japan	$775,689	61.9%
Foreign	478,220	38.1
Total	$1,253,909	100.0%
Income taxes current:		
Japan	$491,614	71.2%
Foreign	198,757	28.8
Total	$690,371	100.0%

Source: Wheeler (1990).

harmonisation, except that the basis of inter-segment pricing need not be disclosed, and the term "net assets" is not necessarily consistent with segment "identifiable assets" under FAS 14 or "assets employed" as under IAS 14. The latter recommendation of the International Accounting Standards Committee, issued in 1981, also requires the basis of transfer pricing to be disclosed. Hence, SSAP 25 need not necessarily result in greater comparability and the UK, in common with all EC countries, has adopted the "seriously prejudicial" clause, which can be a means of avoiding segmental disclosure entirely (Emmanuel and Garrod, 1992).

Other transnational pronouncing bodies have recommended that international transfer pricing should follow the "arm's-length" principle. This is the price which unrelated parties would charge and accept in a transaction: or it is the price that results from an uncontrolled taxpayer dealing at arm's length with another uncontrolled taxpayer. Both the UN (1978) and the OECD (1979) have supported this principle, and by establishing an international consensus, the significance of the issue has been highlighted. However, the pronouncement to follow the arm's-length principle is merely a recommendation. Different national governments and MNEs have been able to interpret it differently with some degree of satisfaction, which may explain its enduring quality. At the specific level of agreement on common criteria or common rules, little progress appears to have been made (Picciotto, 1992).

There is little doubt that these transnational bodies and their forerunner, the League of Nations, recognised international transfer pricing as

TABLE 4.3 Segment information published in the US 20-F filing by Beazer plc

	1986		1987		1988	
			Year ended 30 June			
Net sales:						
Homes and property	248.9		366.3		488.3	
Contracting	195.6		441.4		569.2	
Building materials	1.6		156.5		247.3	
Discontinued						
operations	61.0		68.8		38.5	
	507.1		1,033.0		1.343.3	
Geographical analysis of						
net sales:		%		%		%
United Kingdom	470.8	93	751.9	72.2	896.5	67
United States	25.4	5	234.2	22.6	352.4	26
Others	10.9	2	46.9	4.5	94.4	7
	507.1	100	1,033.0		1,343.3	
Income before income						
taxes, minority						
interests & extra-ordinary						
items:						
Homes and property	30.1		46.9		82.7	
Contracting	7.5		11.6		11.1	
Building materials	0.2		19.4		29.2	
Discontinued						
operations	3.3		8.4		3.2	
Total trading profit:	41.1		86.3		126.2	
Corporate overhead	(0.9)		(1.5)		(3.3)	
Earnings from						
operations:						
Net interest	40.2		84.8		122.9	
	(9.5)		(18.4)		(20.6)	
Related companies	–		2.6		3.7	
Other income	31.1		3.3		8.7	
	31.1		72.3		114.7	
Geographical analysis of						
net income:		%		%		%
United Kingdom	26.6	85.6	40.8	56.4	79.1	68.9
United States	2.5	8.0	25.2	34.8	33.0	29.0
Others	2.0	6.4	6.3	8.8	2.6	2.0
	31.1		72.3		114.7	

TABLE 4.3 Continued

	1986		Year ended 30 June 1987		1988	
Depreciation:						
Homes and property	0.9		1.4		2.1	
Contracting	3.4		8.4		10.9	
Building materials	0.1		10.4		15.1	
Discontinued operations	2.0		2.1		1.4	
	6.4		22.3		29.5	
Net book value of identifiable tangible fixed assets:						
Homes and property	41.2		54.1		55.6	
Contracting	33.1		45.9		56.1	
Building materials	4.4		264.2		264.7	
Discontinued operations	21.0		9.2		–	
Corporate office	–		–		2.1	
	99.7		373.4		378.5	
Geographical analysis of tangible fixed assets:		%		%		%
United Kingdom	95.2	96	98.4	27	98.5	26
United States	2.4	2	263.4	70	267.2	71
Others	2.1	2	11.6	3	12.8	3
	99.7		373.4		378.5	
Capital expenditure:						
Homes and property	5.0		18.0		7.6	
Contracting	6.0		17.4		21.5	
Building materials	2.0		8.1		22.2	
Discontinued operations	3.0		4.5		3.3	
Corporate office	–		–		2.1	
	16.0		48.0		56.7	
Average number of persons employed by the group:						
Homes and property	1,979		2,269		2,734	
Contracting	3,709		8,068		9,818	
Building materials	86		2,225		3,337	
Discontinued operations	1,641		948		1,005	
Corporate office	23		30		32	
	7,438		13,540		16,926	

TABLE 4.4 Segment report published in the United Kingdom by Beazer plc

	Turnover		Profit	
	1988 *£m*	*1987* *£m*	*1988* *£m*	*1987* *£m*
Homes and property	488.3	366.3	82.7	46.9
Contracting	569.2	441.4	11.1	11.6
Building materials	247.3	156.5	29.2	19.4
Discontinued operations	38.5	68.8	___	___
	1,343.3	1,033.0		
Trade profit			126.2	86.3
Central costs			(3.3)	(1.5)
Operating profit			122.9	84.8
Geographical analysis of turnover and operating profit:				
United Kingdom	896.5	751.9	81.7	48.8
United States of America	352.4	234.2	38.4	25.9
Others	94.4	46.9	2.8	10.1
	1,343.0	1,033.0	122.9	84.8

a potentially explosive political issue. At one extreme, it could be used to minimise or avoid taxes, while at the other, it could expose MNEs to overlapping or double taxation, with grave consequences for international trade. Adherence to the arm's-length principle at least gave the appearance of an international accord. However, inconsistent accounting disclosure requirements result in our information about international transfer pricing being imperfect and incomplete. It therefore appears that it will be many years before the harmonisation of financial accounting disclosure requirements provides an effective constraint over MNEs' choice of transfer pricing practice.

NATIONAL GOVERNMENT POLICIES

It is often argued that host governments can introduce legislation and other constraints to restrict MNEs' discretion over the setting of transfer

TABLE 4.5 Comparison of segment ratios under UK and USA disclosure requirements: Beazer plc

Profit margin by geographical segment	UK operations		US operations		Other operations	
	1987	1988	1987	1988	1987	1988
Under UK disclosure	6.5%	9.1%	11.1%	10.9%	21.5%	3.0%
Under US disclosure	5.4%	8.8%	10.8%	9.4%	13.4%	2.8%
Rate of return on investment (ROI) Under US disclosure	41.5%	80.3%	0.02%	12.4%	54.3%	20.3%
Sales:investment Under US disclosure	764.1%	910.2%	88.9%	131.9%	404.3%	737.5%

prices. It should also be recognised that governments provide incentives for MNEs to locate or trade with their individual countries. These incentives create market imperfections which may be exploited by international transfer pricing, and by so doing, MNEs are responding rationally to government-created differentials.

The literature relating to foreign direct investment highlights the importance of securing ownership, location and internationalisation advantages (Leitch and Barrett, 1992). Consistent with Porter's (1980) competitive advantage, MNEs can adapt vertical integration and distribution networks which give credit, scale and knowledge benefits. Transaction cost imperfections in global markets are therefore apparent to MNEs, transfer prices being one of the ways in which they can be exploited (Dunning and Rugman, 1985).

The determinants of foreign direct investment can be influenced by host government policies. For example, the ownership of capital assets in a particular country may confer a competitive edge, and liberal write-offs for tax purposes may provide the justification for selecting a certain country. Cooperative national government policies in terms of tax moratoriums, industrial relations and wage negotiation mechanisms, for example, may influence location advantages. Internationalisation advantages may depend on a host government's ability to ensure stable supplies and a generally stable economic-political environment. In practice, virtually all host governments provide some incentive to encourage foreign direct investment, thereby creating market imperfections. In Japan, for example, there appears to be an export incentive scheme which allows up to a 90% write-off of the cost of investment in a foreign subsidiary against Japanese taxes.

EXAMPLE 4.1

Double deduction of export costs

Japanese parent		US subsidiary	
Investment in US	$100m.	Inventory	$100m.
		Sales	70m.
Export cost		Loss available for	
deduction		carry forward in	
$(0.5^* \times 90)$	45m.	US	30m.
Net cost of			
investment	55m..		

*Assumes Japanese tax rate of 50%

Comparison of the net cost of investment and US sales reveals that $15m. excess cash has been received or saved. This permits the parent to make a profit by the subsidiary selling at a loss (Wheeler, 1988).

Other examples include the Irish government's tax moratorium on exports, and differential tax rate changes as between Puerto Rico and the USA. Each host government incentive to influence the foreign direct investment decision may create a market imperfection which transfer pricing is sufficiently versatile to exploit.

Several surveys of managerial perception of important market imperfections or environmental factors have been undertaken (Leitch and Barratt, 1992). By and large, these indicate that national government policies are influential, particularly those policies which attempt to limit MNE discretion. For example, from 290 responses from large, UK manufacturing and mining companies, Tang (1982) found:

- government restrictions and cash flow for foreign subsidiaries;
- customs duties, anti-dumping and monopoly legislation;
- inflation and currency fluctuations;
- royalty and management fee restrictions and local partner interests;
- relationship with host countries;
- performance evaluation of subsidiaries

to be the most important factors. A later study in the USA (Tang, 1992) gave similar findings. Al-Eryani, Alam and Akhter (1990) confirm the significance of legal constraints, but suggest these are most important when the size of the firm is recognised. The influence of external pressures appears to be a function of size and the proportion of exports sent to subsidiaries, according to Burns (1980), but the internal foreign environment, cash flow, artificial barriers, taxes and economic structure are also influential.

One potential area of controversy is the issue of whether MNEs use the same records for tax and performance evaluation purposes. Whilst not the only explanation, maintaining two systems may suggest that market imperfections exist and are sufficiently great to merit the extra costs of administration. Yunker (1983) found that MNEs which place emphasis on overall global profit used alternative measures of profit to evaluate subsidiary managers – the implication being that one transfer pricing method was used for tax and for internal reporting purposes. This finding is supported by Czechowicz, Choi and Bavishi (1982) in their survey. However, Borkowski (1992), from a sample of seventy-nine US MNEs, found that 66% kept dual sets of books. This may reflect the real difficulties associated with one transfer price serving several roles. By implication, it suggests that market imperfections are significant. Borkowski also found that the majority of companies surveyed used cost-based transfer prices. This raises a further question: can MNEs, within their regulated environments, nevertheless justify the manipulation of their transfer pricing practices?

At one level, this may require the fiscal agencies' acceptance of some form of cost-oriented price. At a more subtle level, the MNE through its own production and sales decisions may induce market forces to create advantageous prices. Researchers have produced economic models to show how changes in tariff regulations can result in advantages through transfer price adjustments (Eden, 1983) and how tax differentials can be exploited (Jensen, 1986). Prusa (1990) takes the view that host governments have regulatory powers limited to quantity and price controls, tax and repatriation restrictions which cannot influence all activities of an MNE. Prusa advocates a flexible application of government regulations, otherwise MNEs will be capable of exploiting global market imperfections. Hence, if an artificially high transfer price is charged, the host country should respond by lowering the number of units the MNE can sell.

Acknowledgement of market imperfections being a major reason for the comparative advantage of MNEs suggests that national government policies cannot be developed in isolation. Within the host country, repatriation, tariff, tax and other policies must be recognised as interrelated, and where feasible, related to other national governments' policies. Each unilateral incentive or restriction developed by national governments increases imperfection in the global market. Far from preventing advantageous transfer pricing manipulation, unco-ordinated government policies may create the environment in which they become essential.

Fiscal agencies

Due to the apparent lack of co-ordination of government policies within and across borders, it is unlikely that any one set of regulations will effectively curtail aggressive transfer pricing. However, the fiscal agencies are probably the best-experienced players to exercise some countervailing power.

Rules to prevent aggressive transfer pricing were introduced in 1915 in the UK, in 1917 in the USA, in 1925 in Germany and in 1933 in France (Picciotto, 1992). Beginning with the League of Nations reports (1932, 1933) and subsequently, the OECD and UN, a degree of international consensus was reached insofar as the arm's-length principle for transfer pricing was adopted. But this largely came about as a response to the double-taxation problem.

The OECD Model Convention (1977) permits adjustments to the profits of an enterprise where, in dealing with related enterprises, "conditions are made or imposed between the two enterprises in their commercial or financial relations which differ from those which would be made between independent enterprises" (Article 9.1). If an adjustment is made by one country's fiscal agency, the Convention calls for the other contracting state to make an adjustment to the profits of the enterprise in its jurisdiction to take into account the first state's adjustments. If differences of opinion arise between the two states, the Convention calls for the competent authorities of the respective jurisdictions to consult with one another. Article 9 of the UN Model Double Taxation Convention follows the same approach and both Conventions substantiate the arm's-length principle. Whilst the OECD Convention was originally intended for bilateral exchange of information, discussion of multilateral exchange involving the twenty-four full member states has taken place. If agreed, the information exchanges could be routine, spontaneous, specific, industry-wide or simultaneous. The last of these would allow both fiscal agencies to share information on a specific cross-border transaction. The USA has simultaneous examination agreements with seven industrial countries, including the UK, and it may be just a matter of time before other tax authorities adopt such measures or the OECD produces a multilateral information exchange agreement. Hence, there is an international structure for dealing with the double-taxation problem which embodies the arm's-length principle. The difficulty arises in making the principle operational.

The OECD (1979) recommended three methods of pricing which were consistent with the principle:

1. *Comparable uncontrolled price*, where independent parties are trading in similar circumstances in the same or very similar goods and where their price is readily verified.
2. *Resale price method*, which deducts from the price paid by an independent party for the final product, an appropriate mark-up to cover that part of the seller's expenses and to generate a reasonable profit.
3. *Cost-plus method*, which adds a suitable mark-up on the cost to the selling subsidiary or division.

The Internal Revenue Service of the USA has followed this same list of preferences for many years (Section 482) and, in addition, accepts a fourth method for transactions covering tangible goods and property. If the three specified methods cannot be applied, some other appropriate method can be used. However, the MNE bears the burden of proof in demonstrating the soundness of any of these "fourth" methods.

For services, the IRS indicate that the charge for the same or similar services in independent transactions with or between unrelated parties under similar circumstances, considering all relevant facts, should form the basis of the arm's-length price. This is repeated for intangible property, except that twelve factors may be taken into account, including prevailing rates in the industry, offers of competitors and prospective profits to be generated by the intangible. Hence, for services and intangibles like brands, no specific guidance is available. Up to 1988, the idea of "safe havens" or harbours – prices or profits which fall within a tolerable range – was rejected. This was due partly to the extraordinary range of returns earned at arm's-length within a single industry or company, and partly because the safe havens would act as a "floor", applying only to those MNEs unable to document a more advantageous pattern of facts (US Treasury White Paper, 1988).

The UK Inland Revenue is less specific as to the methods acceptable for "arm's-length" pricing, although since 1915 there has been a provision to charge a foreign parent tax on the basis of a percentage of the turnover of the business undertaken by the UK subsidiary (Taxes Management Act, 1970). Section 485 of that Act gives the Revenue power to adjust the taxable income of the UK party to the figure that would have resulted if the prices actually used had been between two unrelated parties, that is, the arm's-length price. These powers are now contained in the Income and Corporate Taxes Act 1988, s.770. It appears that in principle, an adjustment to the transfer price is required in order to recompute income or profit.

This last point is significant. It highlights a continuing debate between fiscal agencies and MNEs, namely whether tax assessments for distinct segments of an MNE should be determined by the validity of the arm's-length principle applied to specific transactions, or whether the consolidated income of the MNE should be apportioned to the contributing parts. This is our concern over the next chapter.

There is little doubt that fiscal agencies like the Inland Revenue and Internal Revenue Service have the power to investigate MNEs' transfer pricing practices. There is general agreement that the arm's-length principle should apply. However, the criteria and common rules for applying the principle, especially for services and brands, are just not available. The effectiveness of agency investigations is therefore open to question, but as we will see in Chapter 5, this is changing.

SYNOPSIS

International transfer pricing appears to affect a significant proportion of world trade and, hence, the balance of payments of individual nation states. The exact dimensions are unclear, because financial disclosure regulations are not harmonised. Segmental disclosure is even more fragmented. The growth of MNEs and foreign direct investment may be viewed as a logical economic consequence of global market imperfections. These may be caused by national governments providing incentives for MNEs, or attempts to restrict the discretion of MNEs. The net result in either case is the same with tax and tariff differentials, different repatriation rules, etc., providing MNEs with the opportunity to increase their comparative advantage through transfer price adjustments. Double taxation agreements and conventions like those of the UN and the OECD give fiscal agencies the opportunity and power to investigate pricing practices. However, attempts to translate the arm's-length principle into an operational set of rules which can be universally accepted have floundered. Certainly up to 1988, the ability of the accounting regulators, national governments and fiscal agencies to constrain MNE discretion over cross-border pricing appears to have been limited. These are not the only players, of course, as anti-trust officials, customs officials, investors, creditors and trade unions (Arpan, 1972) may all have a real interest in the pricing policies of MNEs. However, it is difficult to gauge how these interested parties may exert influence where accounting regulators, national governments and fiscal agencies have failed.

QUESTIONS

1. Examine the segment report of any UK listed company and conduct a similar analysis to that contained in this chapter. Attempt to explain the results without referring to transfer pricing policies.

2. For a sample of ten UK listed companies chosen at random, discover how many comply with IAS 14 and SSAP 25 or invoke the seriously prejudicial clause. Discuss and interpret your findings.
3. Identify causes of global market imperfections, giving real-life examples where possible. By concentrating on one real-life example, explain the potential impact on MNE transfer pricing policy.
4. "Market imperfections will never be overcome until transnational agreement on tariffs, taxes and repatriation issues are resolved". Discuss.
5. What is the relationship between double taxation agreements and international transfer pricing?
6. Why cannot the same method of pricing be used for services, intangible and tangible properties?
7. Outline the goals of national governments and their fiscal agencies. Identify how these may conflict and describe the consequent impact on MNE discretion to set transfer prices.

5

The MNE Perspective

INTRODUCTION

To this point, the ambitions MNEs may hold for cross-border pricing have only been alluded to. In contrast to the domestic situation, where economic allocations of resources and behavioural aspects of performance evaluation are important, considerations of financial and treasury management and justification of foreign direct investment are additional significant issues for international transfer pricing. The multiple roles transfer pricing may play often conflict, and these inherent tensions, or trade-offs, may provide a more effective constraint on MNEs adopting aggressive pricing strategies than any influence exercised by external agencies. However, one fiscal agency is actively considering the introduction of ways in which consolidated profits may be apportioned to the segments of the MNE. This approach would automatically reduce the concern associated with "arm's-length" pricing. It is, however, an approach which is mirrored in the domestic situation where allocations have been branded "incorrigible". Applying such an approach in the international setting could be a highly political issue.

INTERNATIONAL TRANSFER PRICING ROLES

Apart from the economic and behavioural performance aspects found in the domestic situation, international transfer pricing can be used as an integral part of MNEs' financial or treasury management policy. Some of the major considerations in setting transfer prices are:

1. concentration of cash centrally;
2. minimisation of global tax liability, including customs and excise taxes;
3. reduced exposure to risks of inflation and exchange rate fluctuations;
4. avoidance of repatriation of dividends restrictions;
5. improved competitive advantage by providing "cheap" finance;
6. management of joint ventures involving foreign partners;
7. maintaining good relations with host countries and the public in general;
8. provision of relevant performance measures for segments of the enterprise.

(Daniels, Ogram and Radebaugh, 1976)

Pursuing these roles will bring the MNE under the gaze of national governments, fiscal agencies, consumers, foreign partners and their own subsidiary management (Shulman, 1969). The national or host government interest may be further disaggregated to treasury officials, anti-trust and monopolies officials, anti-dumping officials and central statistics officers. The hypothetical MNE, Multikorp Inc., suggests some of these potential transfer pricing roles and whether a relatively high or low charge would be beneficial to the parent company. The direction of the product and service flows are given in Figure 5.1, along with the significant characteristics of the location of each subsidiary. In practice, the choice of relatively high or low transfer price will not be unambiguous.

For example, if the UK subsidiary supplied the South Korean subsidiary, a high transfer price might ensure tax savings but cause the Korean subsidiary to incur financing costs at disproportionately high rates. This

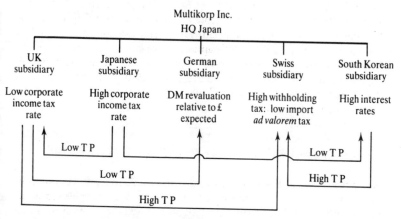

FIGURE 5.1 Potential roles of transfer pricing

Transfer Pricing

ambiguity may provide the most effective safeguard against MNE aggressive manipulation of prices. Even with an apparent straightforward case such as the Japan–UK trade in Multikorp, the decision to price relatively low is not necessarily in the enterprise's best interests.

OPPORTUNITIES AND CONSTRAINTS

Income tax differentials between countries provide MNEs with the opportunity to minimise their global tax liability. With corporate income tax rates higher in Japan than the UK, any cross-border trade where Japan is the supplier suggests that a low transfer price is merited. A transaction in the opposite direction indicates that a relatively high transfer price would be beneficial. The data in Example 5.1 attempt to illustrate this.

EXAMPLE 5.1

Multikorp Inc. Japan–UK trade

	Low TP (millions)	High TP (millions)	
Japan (supplier)			
Revenue/transfer price	1,400	1,800	
Cost of goods sold	1,000	1,000	
Gross profit	400	800	
Other expenses	100	100	
Income before taxes	300	700	
Income tax at 50%	150	350	200 tax
Income after tax	150	350	saving

	Low TP (millions)	High TP (millions)	
UK (purchaser)			
Revenue	2,500	2,500	
Cost of goods sold	1,400	1,800	
Gross profit	1,100	700	
Other expenses	100	100	
Income before taxes	1,000	600	
Income tax at 30%	300	180	120 extra tax
Import duty at 10%	140	180	40 tax saving
Income after tax	560	240	

The assumptions are made that income tax in Japan is 50% and in the UK 30%, where there is also an *ad valorem* import duty or tax of 10%. When a low transfer price is employed, combined income after tax is greater, that is, 710 as opposed to 590 millions. The low transfer price enables the Japan subsidiary to save 200 million in tax and although this is partially offset by the 120 million extra in the UK, there is a net benefit.

The income tax benefit due to the choice of transfer price can be shown in a useful algorithm:

$$TS = (P_2 - P_1)(t_1 - t_2) \qquad \text{(Lin } et\ al., 1993)$$

where TS is the maximum income tax saving in total; P_2 is the high transfer price; P_1 is the low transfer price; t_2 is the income tax rate in the receiving country; t_1 is the income tax rate in the supplying country.

With our data this becomes

$$TS = (1,800 - 1,400)(0.5 - 0.3)$$
$$= 80 \text{ millions}$$

that is, the net effect of the savings at Japan and extra tax at the UK associated with the choice of the low transfer price. Lin *et al.* (1992) demonstrate an extension to take into account income tax rate differences on existing and cross-border transactions:

$$TS = (P_2 - P_1)(t_1 - t_2) + (TI - P_1Q)(t_1 - t_2)$$

As long as the supplying country's income tax rate is greater than the rate in the receiving country, a reduced transfer price will benefit the enterprise, *ceteris paribus*.

The Japan–UK trade also recognises import duty tax. At 10%, this provides a further saving when the low transfer price is used. However, at 50%, the saving associated with the low transfer price deteriorate dramatically and absolute income after tax for the UK subsidiary is zero. Some countries purposely charge high *ad valorem* import duties to counterbalance the reduced income tax rates which are employed. There is something of a spiral here. The lower the transfer price, the more likely import duty rates are to be raised or the transfer price questioned; further reduction of the transfer price may invoke anti-dumping legislation.

If d_2 is the *ad valorem* import duty, then import duty saving (IDS) is depicted as:

$$IDS = (P_2 - P_1)d_2$$
$$= (1800 - 1400)0.1$$
$$= 40 \text{ million duties saved}$$

The relationship between income tax and import duty is more

complicated if the duty is included as a cost in computing income before taxes. This affects the extra income tax in the UK, resulting in the additional cost of the low transfer price being 132 million (258m. under low, compared with 126m. under the high transfer price).

A third form of taxation is withholding tax (WTS) which can be imposed on dividends, interest and royalty payments to the parent. In the UK–Japan trade, the low transfer price allows a significantly higher income after taxes to be reported, but if the UK employed a high withholding tax, the merits of the low transfer price may be justifiably questioned. If:

$$TS + IDS > WTS \qquad \text{(Lin et al., 1992)}$$

the search for an advantageous price by the MNE seems merited, except that there are other, less easily quantified considerations. These include currency fluctuations and inflation, joint ventures and profit repatriation.

Faced with a prospective weakening in the currency of the supplying country, a low transfer price will allow the exchange risk to be hedged. Alternatively, if a strengthening of the supplying country currency is expected, leading the income by means of a high transfer price seems appropriate. The use of "leads and lags" in intra-company international payments has been argued to cause currency instability (Governor of Bank of England, 1973). Assume in Example 5.1 that all the financial data is expressed in yen, and although the current exchange rate is ¥270–£1, a revaluation of the yen is expected. Converting the UK subsidiary's results to sterling and adjusting for a 37% revaluation in the yen renders the choice of transfer price superfluous.

EXAMPLE 5.2

UK subsidiary income after tax

	Low TP	High TP
1. Expressed in Yen	¥560m.	¥240m.
2. Expressed in £ sterling (¥270–£1)	£2.07	£0.89
3. Expressed in Yen (¥170–£1)	¥351.9	¥151.3
Japan income after tax	¥150	¥350
	¥501.9	¥501.3

A 37% revaluation may be unusual, but the impact of ignoring foreign exchange fluctuations cannot be under-estimated. The advantages of a particular transfer price can be enhanced or destroyed unless the currency risk is managed properly.

When the currency is not convertible or controlled, the scope for foreign exchange management is constrained. A high transfer price is required in order to reduce the risk and to avoid problems in repatriating profits. In general, a high transfer price is recommended to overcome profit repatriation constraints imposed by host governments which lack foreign currency reserves or suffer balance of payments problems. At the extreme, the threat of nationalisation of overseas subsidiaries may direct MNEs to seek an early return on their investments, by overpricing intra-company transactions. Where the economic-political environment is more stable and the subsidiary represents a new investment in that country, a policy of under-pricing or low transfer pricing may provide a competitive advantage to gain a foothold in that market. This policy can also be used to avoid high financing costs in the host country. A low transfer price improves the cash flow of the newly established subsidiary.

The form of the overseas investment may also influence the transfer pricing policy. Joint ventures are increasingly common and developments in China and the former Soviet Union have resulted in many MNEs adopting this form of enterprise as a means of entry to new markets. In respect to transactions involving the joint venture and the MNE, the choice is simple. Use of a high transfer price on in-bound transactions ensures the MNE achieves an early return and a higher proportion of the profits. A lower transfer price would result in higher joint venture profits in which the MNE can claim only a portion. However, the adoption of the over-pricing policy requires the agreement of the board of directors of the joint venture and may not be easily obtained.

Use of the joint venture, the recognition of currency fluctuations, competitive strategy and profit repatriation issues are less easily quantified, but can have an influence over the ultimate choice of transfer price. The fact that not all these roles can be fulfilled simultaneously probably provides the most effective constraint on aggressive over- and under-transfer pricing. Managerial performance evaluation potentially provides a further limitation to aggressive pricing behaviour.

PERFORMANCE EVALUATION

Distinctions between the performance of the manager and that of the subsidiary are rarely found, in practice (Vancil, 1979; Coates *et al.*, 1993). Reports internal to the MNE will incorporate transfer pricing data as revenues and costs for the respective parties to a transaction. Hence, if managers perceive that their well-being is affected due to the transfer price influence on profit performance, their behaviour in this respect is likely to be influenced. When managerial incentive schemes are based, even in part, on financial performance measures, it is an unusual (possibly

brave, possibly foolhardy) manager who will not actively seek to influence transfer pricing policy. Chapters 6 and 7 of this book deal with
these issues in detail. Here, we will examine why managers of separate
subsidiaries may not be indifferent between over- or under-pricing of
cross-border transactions. If this is the case, subsidiary management may
provide a further constraint on MNEs exercising total discretion.
Although examples of "whistle-blowing" by managers are rare, the
occasions when they happen, as in the cases of Hoffmann La Roche
(UK Monopolies Commission, 1973) and New York's Citibank (Dale,
1984), create such tumultuous reactions that MNEs cannot easily discount them. The data in Example 5.1 are again used to illustrate
the impact of transfer pricing policy on managerial and subsidiary
performance.

EXAMPLE 5.3

Managerial and subsidiary performance

	Absolute profit	*ROI*	*Residual income (RI)*
Low transfer price			
Japan	150	15%	50
UK	560	56	460
High transfer price			
Japan	350	35%	250
UK	240	24	140

Each subsidiary is assumed to have an investment base of 1,000 millions
and for residual income purposes, a cost of capital of 10%.

The Japanese subsidiary outperforms the UK subsidiary for all financial
performance measures when a high transfer price is charged. The relative
performance reverses when a low transfer price is used. Whilst total
enterprise income after tax changes with the choice of transfer price (low
710, high 590), the significant changes in reported income occur at the
subsidiary level. A change of less than 30% in the value of the transfer
price can result in the UK's absolute profit and ROI measures being
reduced by more than half and RI falling by almost 70%. The magnifi-
cation effect of the change in transfer price is obvious. If these financial
performance measures are perceived by the managers as being personally
important, we cannot expect them to be indifferent between the choice
of transfer price. Evaluation in local or parent currency and against bud-
gets which include projected rate changes or closing rates enhance or

diminish managerial concern with transfer pricing (Lessard and Lorange, 1977). The variability of subsidiary results depends on the range of feasible transfer prices. In the Japan–UK example, a change of just under 30% was assumed. Lin *et al.* (1992) refer to a Harvard Business School case on John Deere to demonstrate that a change of costing system from, say, allocating costs by labour or machine hours to activity-based costing, can result in deviations of 30%. A legitimate change in costing system can therefore justify a wide range of cost-based transfer prices.

Yunker's survey (1982) categorised certain transfer pricing methods as more likely to under-price then over-price. Virtually all cost-based transfer prices, except actual or standard full cost plus a fixed mark-up, are believed to lead to under-pricing. Full cost plus, negotiated and market-oriented transfer prices tend to over-price. Even if these tendencies exist, subsidiary management are nevertheless likely to try to influence the price in their individual best interest. The problem of information asymmetry and the maintenance of decentralisation are still present in the international context and subsidiary managers are just as likely to manipulate data as their domestic divisional counterparts. Perhaps the greatest difference is that by allocating profit efficiently in the global setting, the rewards for the MNE are significantly greater than in the domestic context. Objections by subsidiary management that financial performance measures no longer reflect independent success or failure may count for little when viewed from a global perspective. The trade between two subsidiaries may be just the start of some elaborate network of deals which will benefit the MNE ultimately.

This degree of complexity is best exemplified by the transnational financial intermediaries which operate in the global financial markets. With the high volume of transactions, speed of transacting and the importance of a margin of a fraction of 1%, bilateral and "transfer pricing" deals are built on to create sophisticated networks of movements of currency, cash and credit (Picciotto, 1992). Bank regulators and fiscal authorities have the power to investigate transfer pricing practices, but there is no single market and no universally recognised market rate. Examination of one deal in isolation may not indicate the eventual benefits. Bartlett (1981) cites Edwards of New York's Citibank as stating that "in order to get a full picture of a Citibank interbank transaction, it is necessary to examine its individual components at all branches involved" (p. 110). Identifying separate transactions and even separate, distinct parts of an enterprise have been undermined by the internationalisation of markets and day-long, continuous availability to traders. The concept of monitoring transfer pricing arrangements for individual cases appears close to inoperable. The question arises as to why transfer prices should be investigated if they are employed to benefit the MNE in total. Why not accept whatever practices are applied, but base tax charges for an individual subsidiary on a portion of the consolidated income?

Arm's-length price or arm's-length profit

Adoption of the arm's-length principle requires fiscal authorities and others to examine the prices of specific transactions, wherever possible using comparable prices between unrelated parties. One alternative approach is to allocate global profit to segments or subsidiaries of the enterprise. This latter approach requires comparison with the profits of other similar undertakings to be available. The arm's-length profit or profit-split principle may not be easily applied, however.

Local companies report profit in terms of the national generally accepted accounting principles, which are unlikely to accord with the MNE's consolidation practices. Restatement of the local company accounts into the language of the MNE with consistent treatments of off-balance sheet financing, inflation adjustments and accounting for pension costs are just some of the problems to be faced. Even when feasible, the heroic assumptions have to be made that the local company and subsidiary enjoy similar market positions, levels of efficiency and advanced technology.

There is also the considerable doubt that these comparisons may cause disagreements among national tax authorities. The suggested use of "safe havens" which provide ranges of tolerance for prices is based on the expectation of a certain range of profits being made (Picciotto, 1992). However, apart from standard transactions occurring in competitive markets, defining a "safe haven" can be problematic.

For MNE's to accommodate the split profits approach, consolidation of world-wide operations would be needed with the accounts being adjusted for the tax rules of each country of operation. Currency conversion and asset revaluation treatments would require harmonisation, and when completed, each tax authority would apply a formula for allocation of profits to subsidiaries. Double taxation appears distinctly likely. Mirroring the domestic situation, it may appear that the problems of international transfer pricing can be avoided, but only insofar as solving the subsequent allocation conundrum.

Despite the difficulties of operating a split profits approach, there appears to be an underlying contradiction in fiscal agencies focusing on specific transactions whilst MNEs adopt a global strategy to exploit market imperfections. There have also been other developments to tighten or make transparent MNE discretion over international transfer pricing.

DEVELOPING EFFECTIVE CONSTRAINTS

Wheeler (1990, p. 11) states that "it is doubtful if any area has more tax dollars involved than section 482 cases". Yet the Internal Revenue Service record in these tax cases is not very good. Picciotto (1992) argues that, despite the development over two decades of guidelines such as those of the OECD, there is still no effective transfer price regime, and that even sophisticated tax authorities have experienced difficulties in policing taxpayer compliance. This view is echoed by Leitch and Barrett (1992) and all of these writers agree that obtaining transfer pricing information from MNEs is a major stumbling block. Whilst these commentaries relate to the OECD and US attempts to constrain over-aggressive transfer pricing, there is no evidence of which we are aware to indicate that other countries have been more successful in creating more effective safeguards. The administrative difficulties related to obtaining transfer pricing information have been comprehensively reviewed in the US Treasury Section 482 White Paper (1988).

Application of section 482

Questionnaire responses were obtained from selected international examiners and their group managers supplemented by interviews with IRS economists and trial lawyers and other international examiners and group managers. An estimated number of seventy responded.

Just over one-third indicated that the tax notes, segmental reports or other information contained in the annual report of the MNE are considered when identifying or developing a case. When taken further, in almost 75% of the cases the MNE had no readily available information to support the basis of the transfer price transaction. The average delay in responding to IRS requests for information was 12.2 months and delay occurred in over 50% of the reported cases. The reasons ranged from records located overseas to lack of cooperation between parent and subsidiary. In these instances, the IRS international examiners have power to issue a summons to obtain the necessary information. However, this option was exercised in only 5% of cases, because it usually signals the end of future cooperation in domestic audits and can lead to further delays. Not surprisingly, the process of obtaining relevant information can be extremely time-consuming. The ready availability of information may be conditioned by the method of transfer pricing the MNE has adopted and the type of work flow. Table 5.1 indicates these for the reported questionnaire responses.

The MNEs determined comparable pricing bases for services by reference to charges to third parties, sales to 50%-owned subsidiaries, industry norms and several other bases. Only 19% of the IRS examiners accepted

TABLE 5.1 Transfer pricing bases and work flows: IRS investigations

	For services, intangibles	For tangible property, goods
Comparable uncontrolled price	32%	31%
Resale price method	8%	18%
Cost plus method	24%	37%
Other	36%	14%

Source: US Treasury White Paper 1988, pp. 119–22.

the MNE comparable price basis. Reasons for this ranged between the circumstances of service provision being different to that provided to a third party, volumes of the comparable transaction being small, and ignoring the overall transaction effect. Some of the difficulties IRS examiners encountered in developing a comparable transaction themselves included adjustments for different geographic markets, and the problem of acquiring information from third parties, especially concerning transactions five or six years in the past.

For tangible property transactions, over 75% of the reported cases indicate that MNEs rely on a profit split to determine the transfer price. This primarily requires a comparison with the profits of other similar local undertakings, which is not without its difficulties. Strangely, a similar approach is not favoured by MNEs when intangibles are the focus. Cost-sharing on a variety of bases appears to characterise research and development, marketing, trade name and trademark defence costs. Of the respondents, 50% reported cases involving transfers of intangibles, with adjustments being necessitated in half this percentage.

Critical difficulties concerned the ability to identify separately the intangible, document the transfer and value the intangible. Transfer of tangible goods or property or the provision of service often occurs simultaneously with the transfer of intangibles. The tax authorities need to determine the appropriate transfer pricing value when goods are transacted with and without the relevant MNE's logo, for example. This is similar to the equally daunting task of setting a royalty rate for a licensed intangible such as a unique pharmaceutical product. Employee transfers within the enterprise may simultaneously provide services and transfer valuable intangible know-how and thereby expand an already wide-ranging set of bases and values. Providing a common frame of analysis to avoid the tax authorities using one method while the MNE employs another basis appears extremely difficult in the circumstances surrounding intangible transfers. The White Paper recognises that:

In practice, taxpayers and agents rely upon comparable uncontrolled prices or transactions, when they exist. When they do not exist, agents or tax-payers use whatever method they believe best reflects the economic realities of the transaction at issue.

(US Treasury, White Paper p. 19)

It is from this pragmatic stance that the IRS international examiners frequently use functional analysis.

Functional analysis

Functional analysis concentrates on the economic functions performed by the affiliated parties to the transaction and the economic risks which each of the parties bears. It can be used to verify the resale price or cost plus methods, or to provide criteria for justification of the "other" method. Since 1986, the IRS has developed capacity to undertake this analysis and has employed specialist lawyers and economists to assist international examiners. All major transfer pricing cases must involve economists from either the Baltimore, New York or Chicago decentralised offices at an early stage of any investigation.

In an investigation, seven basic questions are addressed by the inter-national examiners and their specialists.

1. What was done?
2. What economically significant function was performed?
3. What economic risk was assumed?
4. Who performed each function and assumed each risk?
5. What is the economic value of each function performed by each party?
6. Were any valuable intangibles used?
7. Who developed the intangibles, and is the developer being paid for their use?

Under functional analysis, profit is apportioned in line with each party's contribution to intangibles, labour and risk involved in the trade. Deter-mination of exactly who earned what is complicated, and the final decision is only obtained by judge or jury. Alternatively, the MNE and fiscal authorities may negotiate a settlement either before a judgment is given or before the case comes to a court. When contested, the burden of proof that the transfer price is reasonable rests with the MNE. The provision of relevant documents, accurate presentation of the facts by a reputable economist and a logical defence of the practice may ensure that judgment is in favour of the MNE.

If a comparable uncontrolled price cannot be adopted, the MNE needs to justify the arm's-length basis of the transfer price by reference to other data. For example, the fiscal authorities questioned the price of sales from a manufacturing subsidiary in a low-tax European country to the parent pharmaceutical company. The company defended its practice by presenting calculations based on the resale price method and a variation of the cost plus method. In both cases, the intangibles were split, marketing associated with the parent and manufacturing with the subsidiary. Under both approaches, the MNE demonstrated that an arm's-length price was being employed. However, MNEs in general may be sensitive to the amount of confidential data required to mount a successful defence. This is borne out by the delay of over a year in responding to IRS requests for information, but this is changing also.

Revenue Reconciliation Act 1990

This US law was introduced in recognition of the difficulties which the IRS faces in obtaining transfer pricing information from MNEs. Non-compliance with IRS requests can result in fines of up to $10,000 per month, with no limits on the cumulative penalty (Pear, 1990). In addition, a 20% penalty can be applied when transfer pricing valuations are mis-stated. This can occur when the transfer price adjustment for a tax year exceeds $10 million of taxable income, or the amount paid for goods or services is 200% or more of the adjusted price. It can also apply when the amount received for goods or services is 50% or less of the adjusted price determined by the IRS. The penalty is progressive, increasing to 40% when, for example, an adjustment of more than $20 million to income is made. When non-compliance occurs, the fiscal authority can decide the appropriate transfer price, a power which the British Inland Revenue also enjoys.

This legislation is therefore trying to rectify at least some anomalies. The original s.482 regulations did not require MNEs to document the methodology used to establish transfer prices, nor to supply this information during an IRS audit. Secondly, the law should remove delays and technically have no adverse affect on the IRS relationship with individual MNEs. Thirdly, the increase in foreign-owned US subsidiaries means that important documents may only be available outside the USA. The introduction of this legislation may therefore be viewed as a significant move to remedy the problems the fiscal authorities have experienced in recent years. Nor have they been slow to use them. At 30 September 1991, $13.6 billion of proposed transfer pricing adjustments were lodged with the Appeals Division (Wright, 1992). Another way the IRS seeks to obtain the relevant information is by making advance pricing agreements attractive to MNEs.

Advance pricing agreements

An investigation or audit by the fiscal authorities is expensive. News that an audit of the financial statements of an MNE is being undertaken can result in the investor community asking questions. In the USA, disclosure of an IRS audit must be made in the annual accounts and report. In addition, the expense associated with external advisers and specialists to defend the transfer pricing practice is not insignificant. Also, the possibility of a transfer pricing adjustment may cause the fiscal authorities to examine other parts of the MNE's operations more closely. Finally, the sums involved inevitably mean that senior management time and effort is devoted to the problem. For these reasons, measures by which to avoid an audit may be attractive, hence the increased use of advance pricing agreements (APAs).

At the MNE's initiative, a transfer pricing method can be agreed with the fiscal authorities to cover a fixed number of years, typically three years. In order to reach agreement, the MNE must provide a similar amount of information as required under a contested audit. Normally this may consist of:

1. a functional analysis of the trade or transaction;
2. an industry analysis to distinguish or compare the product or service with the sector;
3. a financial analysis of the transaction;
4. identification of comparable transactions of goods and services;
5. provision of documents to demonstrate the MNE's arm's-length policy for pricing.

Given the burden, it is not surprising that only forty APAs were negotiated in the USA in early 1992. None the less, for MNEs which may have difficulty in recognising a comparable uncontrolled price, the APA could be a sensible option. In particular, if any subsidiary involved in the transaction should consequently show return on assets, pre-tax gross margins or operating incomes which contradict industry norms, the APA may be beneficial. However, the more common APAs become, the greater the fiscal authorities' knowledge of industry performance comparatives. Given the international nature of the transactions, APAs may only be acceptable when other fiscal authorities are involved. Gradually the case-by-case APAs may allow national industry performance differences or similarities to be identified and help build a body of internationally agreed principles and norms as to acceptable rates of return.

A final potential benefit of APAs is to narrow the gap between the arm's-length approach and a global approach to apportioning profit by formula (Picciotto, 1992). Some APAs appear to allocate both expenses and income by means of a formula agreed by the relevant tax authorities and the individual MNE. This may be regarded as a practical attempt to adopt the arm's-length principle to the realities of complex intra-group trading as it occurs today.

Therefore the changes effecting compliance, functional analysis and APAs can be seen as attempts to enforce and tighten taxation laws, rather than fundamental changes in the rules for determining transfer prices. The OECD, however, takes a different view.

THE OECD AND THE COMPARABLE PROFIT METHOD

On the question of compliance, the Revenue Reconciliation Act and APAs, the OECD (1993) is in broad agreement with the American changes. In fact, the report recognises that APAs are particularly suitable when price determination is difficult and there is a need to agree an allocation of expenses and income in advance. However, the OECD is cautious about any move away from first concentrating on the determination of a price for a specific transaction.

Following the 1988 Treasury White Paper, the US has issued its proposed income tax regulations relating to intercompany transfer pricing and cost-sharing arrangements under section 482 of the Internal Revenue Code. Whilst the comparable uncontrolled price is the preferred basis for both tangible and intangible property transactions, it is the new reliance on the comparable profit method which causes the OECD some unease. This may be used to substantiate the resale price or cost plus methods for tangibles, and as an alternative when the comparable adjustable transaction method cannot be applied for intangibles. In all cases, the comparable profit method would involve testing one of the transacting parties' financial results with those earned by unrelated parties performing similar functions and dealing with similar products.

The comparable profit method consists of six stages:

1. Identification of the subsidiary whose profits are to be compared.
2. Profit comparison with independent or uncontrolled taxpayers whose business closely corresponds with the subsidiary.
3. Profit level indicators of the uncontrolled taxpayers are determined and likely to be expressed in profit to capital investment ratios, such as ROI and ROCE.
4. The chosen profit level indicators are applied to financial data of the subsidiary and a comparable profit interval or range is determined.
5. The most appropriate point within the profit interval is then obtained by considering multiple indicators derived from the uncontrolled or independent parties, possibly using statistical techniques.
6. From the most appropriate point in the profit interval, the transfer price for the controlled transaction is calculated.

The comparison allows for the subsidiary's financial results to be averaged over the current year, the preceding year and the following year. When subsidiary profits fall outside the comparable profit interval, an adjustment is required, although unanticipated and partially overlapping results mitigate against this.

The OECD's concern relates to the fact that price is but one ingredient in determining profit. The validity of the comparisons can only be justified if it accords with commercial realities. Whilst the independent taxpayers may serve similar functions or make similar products, differences in

1. cost structures and systems;
2. geographic locations;
3. quality of management;
4. costs of capital;
5. business efficiency and experience; and
6. corporate objectives

may explain differences in performance more completely than merely an aggressive transfer pricing policy. In addition, "it would *prima facie* be unfair to adjust the profits of an unsuccessful multinational enterprise merely on the grounds that it was not as profitable as its more successful competitors" (OECD, 1993, pp. 22–3). Instead, the profit-split approach is preferred.

This is an internal estimation of what share of the total profits of the group the subsidiary would reasonably be expected to earn at the time of the transaction if it had independent status. The search for external comparables is therefore avoided, as is the need to produce say three years' data. Justification for the eventual profit-split ratio may result from application of a functional analysis. However, functional analysis is not without its costs: the ultimate profit split may be condemned as imprecise or arbitrary, and determination of total profits is difficult if the parent is foreign-owned and subject to different accounting disclosure and reporting regulations.

In some respects the US fiscal authorities' approach and that of the OECD are not truly different. Both prefer the use of the comparable uncontrolled price, because it complies with the arm's-length principle most clearly. When a comparable adjustable transaction for intangibles cannot be obtained – this is normally an independent contractor's price – then, for both intangible and tangible property the US appears to favour the comparable profit method whilst the OECD prefers the profit-split approach.

SYNOPSIS

Within the MNE, transfer pricing can serve many roles, ranging from securing competitive advantage for a newly-established subsidiary to managing foreign exchange currency fluctuations. The benefits to be reaped from efficient management and selection of transfer prices are not trivial, especially in terms of minimising tax liability. However, many of these potential opportunities are difficult to achieve consistently because they conflict. Not least in significance, performance measurement of subsidiaries and their management teams can be distorted, with a possible adverse effect on motivation, behaviour and rewards.

The management style adopted by the MNE and the resulting impact on decentralisation determines whether international transfer pricing is part of a strategic policy. It would seem that MNEs have the scope and discretion to employ aggressive transfer prices to promote global effectiveness, if they so wish. However, the inevitable trade-offs within the enterprise are probably the best safeguard against this. If these competing roles are "managed", then the focus on specific transaction prices appears ineffectual. Adoption of a split-profits or arm's-length profits approach appears more worthwhile.

However, for this approach and others to work effectively, information must be obtained from the MNE. New penalties to punish non-compliance to provide information in a timely fashion have been introduced in the USA. The trend towards APAs is a further attempt to enforce compliance and to improve the transparency of intra-group transactions. The application of functional analysis requires the MNE to justify current practices and to document the methodology employed to establish transfer prices. These developments represent attempts to tighten existing regulations, especially with respect to complying with requests for information.

Of more fundamental concern is the emergence of a US approach which favours the comparable profit method as opposed to the OECD's profit-split method. The latter involves some, possibly arbitrary, disaggregation of consolidated income between the constituent subsidiaries. The former requires a comparison with similar independent enterprises' performance to determine expected individual subsidiary taxable income.

However, holding the international line that the arm's-length principle should apply still appears sustainable, given these developments. The OECD recognises that the status of the proposed US regulations is important in this respect. Even if the comparable profit method is adopted, disruption of international trade can be avoided, should the regulations be recognised as subservient to mutual agreements on double taxation. This pin-points the need to move to an agreed procedure for arbitration between nation states where transfer pricing disputes cannot be solved through mutual agreement procedures. The OECD has a task force currently examining this and other related issues.

Finally, it is worth placing these developments in context. MNEs are ideally placed to take advantage of and create global market imperfections. Up until recently, the most likely constraint on MNE abuse of transfer pricing discretion is argued to be the internal conflicts generated. Currently, transnational and fiscal agencies are actively changing the rules by which acceptable transfer prices can be determined and the relevant information obtained. As in many complex issues, the potential protagonists walk a tightrope. Over-enthusiastic fiscal authorities risk destroying double-taxation agreements and undermining the confidence needed for international trade to grow. Over-aggressive MNEs risk governmental, social and fiscal backlashes, should their transfer pricing practices not comply with some set of agreed guidelines. Currently, the pendulum and initiative begins to swing in the fiscal authorities' favour, but as Chapter 4 suggests, for several years the MNEs may have been in the favoured position. What is certain is that the issue will not disappear. The issue is significant from a global and individual nation standpoint, yet the sensitivity of MNEs in general, governments and fiscal authorities makes objective research and comment extremely difficult. For these reasons, the material in this chapter has a distinctly US bias which will only be rectified when other parties become more willing to divulge their policies and practices.

QUESTIONS

1. When considering whether to charge a relatively high or low transfer price, what factors should an MNE take into account? Choose one example where the choice of transfer price will be likely to create internal conflict.
2. BUSF plc, a large multinational enterprise has a Venezuelan subsidiary which supplies another subsidiary in Italy with intermediate goods and services. A transfer price in the range 2.5–5 millions may be charged for a shipment. Income tax rates are set at 60% in Venezuela and 30% in Italy, where an *ad valorem* import duty of 10% also applies.

   If the aim of BUSF is to minimise its global tax liability, calculate the transfer price needed to achieve this. What other factors should be taken into account before a final decision is made?
3. A revaluation of the lira relative to the Venezuelan cruzeiro is expected. The current exchange rate is 23.50 cr = 1 lira. In the case of BUSF above, re-evaluate the choice of transfer price, assuming the original data to be denominated in cruzeiros and that the new rate of exchange will be 28 cr = 1 lira.

4. With reference to the original data in Question 2, assume that each subsidiary of BUSF has an investment base of 500 millions and the company believes the cost of capital to be 15%. Calculate three financial performance measures for each subsidiary to compare the effect of using a high and low transfer pricing policy for this shipment.

5. Outline the arguments for and against the comparable profit approach and the profit-split approach.

6. Discuss the likely effectiveness of developments to secure MNE compliance with requests for information from fiscal authorities.

7. What is the potential relationship between functional analysis and advanced pricing agreements? Indicate the difficulties in applying the functional analysis.

8. "Given recent developments and pronouncements by the IRS and the OECD, the 'arm's-length' principle can no longer be said to determine international transfer pricing." Discuss.

6

Information Asymmetry and Participation

INTRODUCTION

The transfer pricing system (TPS) is part of the accounting information system (AIS) which is itself an integral part, if not the most important sub-system, of the management information system (MIS). The MIS is the "life-line" for the decision-making process, and more often than not, managers' information needs are satisfied internally, usually by means of the AIS. Management accounting information in particular is essential in the decision-making process for both decision-facilitating and decision-influencing (Demski and Feltham, 1976) or the reduction of ex-ante and ex-post uncertainty (Tiessen and Waterhouse, 1983). These main uses of information affect both the improvement of outcomes and the ex-post monitoring process or the risk-sharing and motivation role. The transition of companies from the centralised structure to the decentralised multi-divisional structure had a great effect on their MIS and AIS as the M-form structure duplicates managerial positions and, hence, requires more elaborate information systems (Rumelt, 1974).

DECENTRALISATION AND THE INFORMATIONAL ROLE OF TRANSFER PRICING

Among the many functions the TPS is designed to fulfil is the provision of information for measuring divisional performance (usually profitability); and decision-making (e.g., make-or-buy; price of final product; output level). As interdependence increases task uncertainty, the information provided by the TPS is vital for risk-sharing and motivation. The informational role of the TPS is thus important because it provides the choice of the particular transfer price. Bierman (1959, p. 430) pointed out that the choice of the method to be used can be made only after the purpose for which the information is to be used is determined. Traditionally, this purpose was driven by financial reporting considerations, but this is no longer the case as companies gradually realise the primary importance of information for managerial planning and control hence the prominent role of management accounting in the modern corporation.

This is most apparent in the large decentralised company which consists of a multitude of autonomous or semi-autonomous divisions operating in different product markets or geographical locations. The growth of organisations into large, diversified companies has led to the adoption of the decentralised organisational structure whereby authority for decision-making is delegated from corporate management to lower level managers. The prime objective of decentralisation is to reduce risk and uncertainty and to increase managerial efficiency by decomposing large problems into smaller ones, capable of solution by semi-autonomous managers who are supposedly motivated to take the best possible decisions.

Demski and Kreps (1982) and Amershi and Cheng (1990) contend that the need for decentralisation arises because divisional management possesses private (and costly) information which the centre or headquarters staff lacks. This contributes to the imperfect monitoring ability of the centre because the lack of relevant information limits the observability of divisional actions and outcomes. Otherwise, if the centre had access to all information so that perfect monitoring of divisional activities was possible at no or minimum cost, then there would be no need for decentralisation. Thus, by shifting the locus of operating decision-making power further down the hierarchy, top management (or the centre) seeks to place the decision close to the realities of the market-place, i.e. where and when the information is generated. This reduces inefficiency by preserving timeliness and encouraging entrepreneurship.

Therefore, it can be deduced that information asymmetry – or information differences between central and divisional management as well as between divisions – is unavoidable in the large company, as divisional managers are better placed to know about their individual divisions' internal and external environments. However, the extent of information asymmetry may be affected by the inadequacy of the company's information structures and communication channels. For example, interdependent division managers may be encouraged to communicate more with each other than with the centre. More seriously, the informational role of the TPS is curtailed when divisional managers withhold or misrepresent their private information because of perceived effects on their performances. These issues are developed below by treating the transfer pricing problem from an agency theory perspective, specifically the economic perspective of agency. The financial branch of agency theory (Barnea, Haugen and Senbet, 1985) is not believed relevant for the present chapter.

There are three economic models of agency, namely the principal–agent model, the transaction costs economics model, and the Rochester model (Baiman, 1990). The principal–agent model focuses on the choice of an ex-ante employment contract between rational principal and agent operating in a world of uncertainty and information asymmetry. Transaction costs economics (TCE) formulates different governance structures for economic exchange, assuming opportunistic behaviour and bounded rationality. TCE was used by Spicer (1988) to develop an organisation model to the transfer pricing process. This will be discussed in Chapter 8. The Rochester model considers the external labour and capital markets as key determinants of the agency relationship. Among these three models, the principal–agent model is more relevant for the purposes of the present chapter, which examines the relationship between the TPS and the performance measurement, evaluation and reward system (PMERS) and how the interface between these two systems is influenced by information asymmetry and human behaviour.

THE PRINCIPAL–AGENT MODEL (PAM)

The principal–agent model (PAM) asserts that an agency relationship is a contractual relationship that exists whenever one party (the principal) engages another party (the agent) to perform some service on their behalf in an uncertain environment. The contract involves delegating some decision-making authority to the agent, who will be compensated for the service performed (Mirrlees, 1976; Jensen and Meckling, 1976; Pratt and Zeckhauser, 1985; and Merchant and Simons, 1986). Both the principal and the agent are assumed to be rational, wealth-seeking utility maximisers, motivated solely by self-interest. Contract is defined as both the explicit (or written) agreement and the implicit bargaining process over outcomes, ways of judging performance and the resulting pay-offs (Fama and Jensen, 1983).

The contracting relationship is thought to bring the conflicting objectives of principal and agent into equilibrium (Alchian and Demsetz, 1972; Baiman, 1982 and 1990; and Kren and Liao, 1988). The principal is assumed to be risk-neutral, whereas the agent is said to be risk-averse and to prefer leisure to work. It should be added that most agency models have so far been limited to a single principal, single agent relationship over a single time period.

What complicates the agency relationship is that the agent (e.g. divisional manager) has the advantage of possessing private information, sometimes of a superior nature, about the tasks he/she performs and from this diffusion of relevant information for decision-making stems the potential for intra-firm conflict. This gives rise to two major problems: adverse selection and moral hazard. Adverse selection can be pre- or post-contract. For example, potential employees may be motivated to misrepresent (or impact) information about themselves when contemplating recruitment. Once in the job, a divisional manager may divert private information for the gratification of selfish interests by taking actions that may be detrimental to corporate objectives. Moral hazard takes places because of the principal's inability to observe perfectly and measure the agent's effort because of the lack of relevant information. The level of moral hazard is affected by the occurrence and magnitude of non-controllable or unpredictable factors caused by the uncertain environment in which the divisional manager operates. This further impedes the principal's ability to observe and evaluate the agent's effort. If there are no clauses in the employment contract, or provisions in the PMERS, to cushion divisional performance from the effect of non-controllable factors, there is an incentive for the better-informed agent to misrepresent his or her private information in order to safeguard self-interests. This non-cooperative behaviour may also be interpreted as an adverse selection problem.

The two agency problems of adverse selection and moral hazard are therefore essentially information-based problems. This indicates that the agency relationship is not cost-free, because of the need to monitor the agent's activities to ensure that the agent – who is considered effort- and risk-averse – fulfils his/her fiduciary responsibility (contained in the employment contract) of aligning his/her interests with those of the principal. Agency costs can be both financial and non-financial, and consist of what may be called (a) unavoidable or necessary costs and (b) avoidable or inefficient contracting costs.

Unavoidable costs are those the principal is bound to incur to prevent the agent from diverging from his/her contractual obligations to the principal. They include such expenses as the cost of the contract itself, the wages, monitoring costs and rewards. Some of these costs are ex-ante, as they precede the outcomes and, in accounting terms, they are treated as fixed or sunk costs. In the presence of internal trade, these costs are implicit in the TPS and the PMERS which are both formal control mechanisms which seek to integrate the company's objectives or the principal's interests. The costs incurred for designing, administering, reviewing and adjusting the TPS and the PMERS are all unavoidable agency costs in these large companies.

What may be defined as avoidable costs are those costs which result from the perceived (and covert) divergence of the agent's actions from the contractual obligations. These costs are avoidable, in the sense that they may result from the wrong selection of employees in the recruitment stage. If the agent engages in some sort of dysfunctional behaviour such as shirking, distorting information or creating and aggravating conflict, this will entail agency costs, as there are losses to the principal whose interests are hindered by the actions of the agent. The losses are not necessarily purely financial, as dysfunctional behaviour affects not only the financial performance but also the social and cultural norms which constitute the internal fabric of the organisation. If corrective actions are taken such as dismissing, transferring, advising or re-training, this is bound to incur costs which could have otherwise been avoided had the right person been selected for the job in the first place.

Since avoidable costs are the likely result of inappropriate agency contracts, their reduced impact requires the proper design of the contract which, in the presence of transfer pricing, must accommodate the effect of the TPS on divisional performance. This implies a reciprocal relationship between avoidable and unavoidable costs, as the existence of the former leads to the revision of the latter. Conversely, avoidable costs can be minimised or eliminated if the unavoidable costs result from properly designed employment contracts, transfer pricing systems and performance evaluation and incentive schemes.

Interdependence and agency relationships

The existing PAM relates to what may be called uni-directional agency relationships, as represented by Figure 6.1 for the M-form company.

In this traditional form, the PAM does not take into account the hierarchical nature of the relationships in the complex organisation. In fact A2 in Figure 6.1 is a sub-agency relationship of A1, as is A3 a double sub-agency of A2 and A1. Both the written and implicit contracts aim at bringing the conflicting interests of sub-unit managers, divisional managers and senior managers in line with the owners' interests. Therefore sub-unit managers are not only the agents of their direct superiors (divisional managers), but also the agents of higher levels in the hierarchy. In other words, the more one travels down the hierarchical structure, the more complicated the principal–agent relationship becomes. Between the two extremes of the structure, the managers play both the roles of principals and agents. For example a divisional manager is the agent of top management and the principal of sub-unit managers. What is also interesting is the diversity of job description and specialisation,

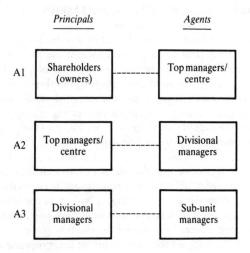

FIGURE 6.1 Uni-directional single agency relationships

personal and managerial objectives, motivation patterns, performance measures and incentive schemes as one travels down the hierarchical structure. In the presence of transfer price transactions, the inter-divisional and intra-divisional trade adds to the complexity of the principal–agent pattern.

The principal–agent model is applied here in the special context of the divisionalised (or hierarchical) company with internal "sales" of goods and services among divisions. The divisionalised structure is characterised by the separation of ownership and control, with divisional managers normally exercising substantial degrees of discretion over operating and other decisions. The information is normally channelled bottom–top, with periodic reports by divisional managers to the centre about divisional and managerial performance. The transfer pricing system plays an important role in this process.

However, it may be argued that since decision-making authority is delegated by the centre to divisions – and not from one division to another – the interaction between divisions caused by the internal trans-action cannot be characterised as a principal–agent relationship. All divisional managers who are party to the transfer transaction are in fact employed by the same company (i.e. the principal) and, therefore, there is no real contractual relationship and no performance evaluation between divisional managers. Moreover, it is unlikely that the clauses of the company's employment contract would specify the transfer pricing rules, though the TPS is an integral part of the management control process. When a transfer price is specified by the centre, the internal transaction may be considered as a mere sale and purchase agreement which does not include any incentive scheme as divisional managers do not have the authority to control, evaluate and reward or penalise each other. Nevertheless, it should be recognised that even if it is not considered as an agency relationship, the internal transaction may be consequential on the results of the parties involved. When divisional or subunit managers have discretion over the setting of a transfer price, this may generate all the behavioural problems identified by agency theory, notably accounting-related incentive conflicts and the costs they entail.

The question that arises from the above argument is whether a formal delegation of authority (and therefore a written contract with specific performance evaluation and reward clauses) is a necessary condition for an agency relationship to exist? In its present state of development, the PAM does not preclude implicit, non-written contracts. The PAM also recognises the effect of uncertainty on outcomes; and because of uncertainty and information diffusion, the principal can only imperfectly monitor the agent's effort. In the case of internal trade, uncertainty is accentuated by the varying degrees of interdependence between and sometimes within divisions.

The existence of internal trade and transfer pricing formalises intra-firm interdependence, which in turn reflects the degree of task uncertainty (Hirst, 1981 and 1983). In other words, the more important and material the internal trade, the higher the degree of task uncertainty and, consequently, the more confused the responsibility boundaries. Moreover, one of the prime objectives assigned to the transfer pricing system is the co-ordination of the production process to fulfil the company's goal function. Stated otherwise, the TPS is sought to align divisional objectives with those of the principal. Thus, the existence of internal trade not only satisfies the tenets of the principal–agent model but it also complicates the agency problems and provides the opportunity to enrich the existing agency theory literature.

Since the PAM is concerned with the design of optimum contractual arrangements whereby the rights and responsibilities of the contracting parties are clearly stipulated, the interactions between and within divisions in the decentralised company in the form of internal transactions are forms of market contract which may be regarded as agency relationships. The transfer pricing agency involves at least three persons: a principal and two agents; the principal being the top management or centre, and the agents being the divisional general managers. In other words, it is a multi-agent situation whose complexity depends, in terms of Dopuch and Drake's (1964) typology, on whether there is internal monopsony, internal monopoly or monopolistic competition; or in terms of Thompson's (1967) typology, on whether the interdependence is pooled, sequential or reciprocal. In a situation of internal monopolistic competition and reciprocal transfers, both the transferor and transferee divisions assume the roles of principal and agent, depending on the direction of the flow of goods and services. Therefore the agency relationship exists at at least two levels of the decentralised hierarchy (Figure 6.2). However, we begin by examining a more straightforward case.

First, there is a company-wide agency between central management and the divisional managers, and second, a divisional level agency between the parties to the internal transaction. One perspective on the divisional relationship is to consider the transferor division as the agent performing services in the form of the supply of intermediate commodities that satisfy the needs of the transferee division or principal. The

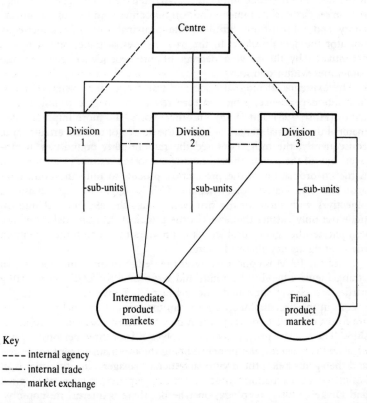

Key
---- internal agency
—·— internal trade
——— market exchange

FIGURE 6.2 Agency relationships in the presence of internal trade in a multi-divisional firm

contract that binds the agency relationship here is the transfer pricing system (TPS) and any informal agreements regarding the transfer transaction. Given that the TPS is part of the management control system, it can be said that transfer prices play both the roles of bonding costs to the transferee and incentives to the transferor. If the transfer transaction is centrally controlled, then the transfer pricing contract is enforced by the imposed administrative process. In this instance, it may be argued that the top management/divisional management relationship dominates and determines the relationship between the divisions. If it is not centrally controlled, the contract is enforced through negotiation which sometimes requires central mediation or arbitration.

The particular transfer price has opposite signs in the objective functions of the divisions and, given the agency theory assumption of motivation by self-interest, the transferor division (agent) will try to maximise its revenue from the transfer, and the transferee division (principal) will try to minimise the impact of the transfer price on its product cost. Consequently, conflict – both overt and covert – arises if either division sees its interests undermined. The situation is complicated when there are restrictions imposed on the divisions by central management and the TPS plays a major role in monitoring divisional performance. In practice, these restrictions may take the form of rules which prevent one division from using the external market until internal demand is satisfied, or a policy which states that only $x\%$ of a particular material may be purchased externally without central management approval. Of course, there are other restrictions imposed by the characteristics of the intermediate good or service which prevent use of the external market as discussed in Chapters 1 and 2. Given the implicit value judgements and behavioural norms inherent in the performance evaluation and reward system, it is normal to expect divisional managers to engage in what may be perceived by central management as dysfunctional behaviour. This may take the form of private information withholding and misrepresentation.

INFORMATION ASYMMETRY AND INCENTIVES FOR PRIVATE INFORMATION DISCLOSURE

Diagnosis of the intricacies of the transfer pricing agency

In multi-agent situations, one or more agents have private or proprietary information that they may use (or rather misuse) to their own personal advantage. Because of the possible conflict between the objectives of the parties to the internal transaction, the divisional manager's response to central management's request of his/her superior information may be depicted as follows:

1. to try to withhold all the superior information, i.e. total non-disclosure;
2. to disclose some of the information, i.e. partial disclosure;
3. to disclose all the information, i.e. voluntary disclosure.

Given the remoteness of the centre (or principal) from the market realities of the individual divisions and the closeness of divisional managers to those realities, the information that the divisional manager may decide to withhold is likely to be that type of information (such as market-based information) that is not usually captured by the accounting information system. For instance, the nature of competition is seen as an important factor in determining the level of disclosure, in that product market competition may provide disincentives for voluntary disclosure (Verrechia, 1983). It should be added here that in the decentralised company, divisional managers and the centre know that information asymmetry exists and, therefore, expect non-disclosure and untruthful disclosure. In other words, the attitudes of the holder of superior information regarding disclosure reflects their perception of the attitudes and reactions of other responsible individuals in the organisation.

As stated earlier the issue of information disclosure in the presence of interdependence becomes more complicated when there are restrictions imposed on the divisions by central management and the TPS plays a major role in monitoring divisional performance. The nature and the structure of the management information system (MIS) are key issues to be addressed by a company when it wants efficient and truthful revelation of relevant information, especially in the presence of divisional linkages. Relying on accounting reports alone does not necessarily produce all the required information.

Moreover, even when private or superior information is partly or totally disclosed, it may either be truthful or impacted. Truthful or bias-free disclosure takes place when the divisional managers (or agents) know or surmise that their self-interests are not undermined. A divisional manager's judgement is normally based on the results of the performance measurement, evaluation and reward system (PMERS) as it is the formal control system by which they are appraised and rewarded. Untruthful or impacted disclosure may also be motivated by short-term interests or the PMERS, like maximisation of divisional profits, return on investment or residual income, and the rewards thereof. The manager's judgement could be a well-informed assessment based, for instance, on past experience or from active participation in decision making; or it may simply be a pessimistic and protective attitude against uncertain outcomes. Therefore the main problem facing the principal is how to motivate the agent to disclose truthfully relevant information – that is to say, what incentives to build in the PMERS to discourage non-disclosure and mitigate information impactedness. Since the transfer pricing issue has, over the last few decades, proved to be one of the thorniest, most complex and puzzling corporate problems (Vancil, 1978; Eccles, 1985a; and Emmanuel, Otley and Merchant, 1990), many factors have to be taken into account in trying to arrive at truth-inducing incentives.

It can now be usefully added that any of the courses of action that the agent might adopt regarding the disclosure of superior information will depend on the perceived costs (and benefits) of disclosure (Table 6.1). A survey by Gray and Roberts (1989) found that at a corporate level, "internal trade" is considered as one of a list of top disclosure items that give rise to the highest costs or lowest net benefits that accrue from information disclosure. From a corporate perspective, the costs of disclosure are not necessarily financial, although they may have an indirect financial result. Examples include loss of established or potential customers and loss of competitive advantage through divulgence of technological particularities. These may be termed "hidden costs".

At a divisional or subordinate level, the agent's perception of the costs of disclosure is, as stated above, essentially influenced by the perceived outcomes of the PMERS. This has as its underlying determinants first, the extent of divisional autonomy (especially over sourcing and pricing) and second, the dimensions of the transfer transaction. In theory, managerial discretion is normally expected in the M-form company

TABLE 6.1 Private information disclosure attitudes

Attitude to disclosure	Nature of information disclosed	Perceived costs of disclosure	Perceived benefits from disclosure
Disclose all	1. all truthful 2. all impacted 3. mixed[a]	Varies	1. TPS advantage and/or 2. PMERS advantage
Withhold all	N/A	1. TPS disadvantage and/or 2. PMERS disadvantage	None
Disclose some and withhold some	1. all truthful 2. all impacted 3. mixed[a]	1. Some TPS disadvantage and/or 2. some PMERS advantage	1. Some TPS advantage and/or 2. some PMERS advantage some truthful and some biased

[a]Some truthful and some biased.

because it is its motivational vehicle, but it must be said that what happens in practice does not always conform to textbook descriptions and prescriptions. For example, particular corporate strategies, such as vertical integration, may impose restrictive policies on divisions and result in the re-centralisation of certain functions that should be delegated to the divisional manager.

Secondly, the dimensions of the transaction include its frequency and size, importance to the division and the company, investment specificity and uncertainty/complexity (Williamson, 1975 and 1986; and Spicer, 1988). In addition to these obvious determinants, human factors such as bounded rationality (or limited abilities) and opportunistic behaviour (Williamson, 1975 and 1986) may also affect the particular course of action. Therefore, the costs of disclosure as perceived by both the principal and the agent affect not only the outcome of the PMERS, but also the inputs to the TPS and the PMERS, such as the determination of the transfer price, the rules for negotiation, the sourcing decision, the make-or-buy decision, the performance measures and the consequent rewards. In sum, the transfer pricing agency is intricate, given the many elements and possibilities involved and, therefore, there is no one best answer to its complex nature. Hence many scenarios can be envisaged (Table 6.2).

Scenario 1: Internal trade non-existent

This is the easiest of cases, as there is no interdependence between divisions and no transfer pricing. This may be the case of non-vertically integrated companies and (conglomerate) companies diversified into unrelated product markets. These companies may be highly differentiated but do not develop strategies of integration, as they do not perceive any benefits from internalising market transactions. The zero-internal trade situation can also be found in companies that prefer subcontracting to making the intermediate product. For example, it is often the case for automobile manufacturers to subcontract the manufacture of vehicle parts from components makers (Monden and Nagao, 1988). This implies that the absence of internal trade does not rule out the existence of intermediate products and markets.

Since there is no intra-company pricing in the zero-transfer case, the TPS–PMERS paradox does not arise and the situation may be characterised as one free from divisional conflict. The agency relationship between top management and individual divisional managers remains, however. Since the PMERS is claimed as one of the important distinguishing features of the M-form company (Williamson, 1975 and 1986), the PMERS on its own may send the wrong signals to divisional managers, who will react by withholding their superior private information. This

TABLE 6.2 Transfer pricing scenarios

Degree of internal trade	Frequency of internal transaction	External intermediate market[a]	Sourcing decision[b]	Transfer pricing decision[c]
Nil	N/A	N/A Exists	N/A	N/A
Negligible	One-off Occasional Recurring	* Exists * Does not exist	* Non-restricted	* Non-mandated[d]
Significant	* One-off * Occasional * Recurring	* Exists * Does not exist	* Non-restricted * Totally restricted * Permission required	* Mandated[e] * Negotiated[f]

Notes: [a,b,c] = Variety of possibilities regarding the existence of external market; the sourcing decision; and the pricing decision, depending on the significance and the frequency of the internal transaction.
[d,e,f] = The transfer price can be based on cost, market or both.

may happen if unlike divisions are pitted against each other through a policy of relative performance evaluation (RPE), especially when there are substantial dissimilarities between divisions in terms of size, amount of allocated resources and the nature of activities. This may also be the case if performance is narrowly and solely evaluated by accounting measures. As accounting data are incomplete measures of performance (Hopwood, 1974; Parker, 1979; and Kren and Liao, 1988), divisional managers may misrepresent the information they possess, in order to secure better rewards for their efforts, or at least to minimise the degree of adversity of the PMERS on their particular divisions. The linkage of rewards to the performance of individual divisions, as opposed to group or a more aggregate measure of performance, may have an influence here.

Scenario 2: Negligible internal trade

Similar to scenario 1, when there is a negligible volume of internal trade – as in the case of a diversified company with unrelated product markets and subcontracting situations – the TPS–PMERS paradox does not arise because there is no significant transfer pricing effect on divisional interests and results. Even if some transfer pricing rules exist for a negligible but recurring amount of transfers, the TPS is unlikely to be a major component of the management control system, nor will it be an element of concern in contractual relationships. Inter-divisional frictions should be minimal due to the availability of alternatives which avoid internal trade. The principal–agent relationships are also well defined, i.e. they are of the first-level or centre–division type and hence, the possibility of diverse divisional interests is limited. Information asymmetry should exist, but the extent of information impactedness is mitigated by the non-materiality of internal trade. Information withholding and untruthful disclosure cannot, however, be ruled out as long as there is accountability and divergence of the interests of the principal and the agents.

Scenario 3: Significant but non-recurring internal trade

Intra-firm trade of significant amounts may take place on a sporadic basis or as a one-off event. Examples of this are:

1. the sudden and temporary disruption of the usual external source of supply;
2. special or one-off large-volume orders;
3. temporary company or divisional policy to force external suppliers to reduce prices and/or meet required quality standards;
4. a company testing the feasibility of different phases of integration, i.e. a cautious transition from a "buy" to a "make" strategy.

These instances imply that intermediate product characteristics are not division-specific and that alternatives are readily available externally. In any of the listed cases, the transfer transaction is not central to the regular activity of the company and the divisions. Therefore, high levels of conflict and information non-disclosure cannot be expected, as the TPS would not have any important or long-term effect on divisional results. It should be pointed out, however, that this reasoning holds true as long as the one-off transaction does not require a special arrangement that may involve altering the existing production and commercial structure of the supplying division. If, however, the internal transaction impedes the normal activity of the division, resulting in the loss of normal business, or requiring extra but non-rewarding effort or investment, it is normal to expect the concerned division to adopt protective measures by way of manipulating private information and/or manifest discontent with the prevailing state of affairs. Such attitudes may become prominent if the one-off investment-specific internal transaction is likely to happen in the future. Nevertheless the divisional manager's ability to withhold information may be limited because the special one-off nature of the transaction allows top management to focus on the precise decision-making needs of the situation.

Scenario 4: Significant and recurring internal trade

When internal trade is part and parcel of a company's business activity, the TPS constitutes a formal integrative, informational and control mechanism. Since the transfer price has opposite signs in the cost and revenue functions of the transferee and transferor, the importance and the frequency of the transaction greatly influence divisional results and behaviours. An appropriate TPS should provide the incentive for voluntary disclosure, but the extent of information disclosure is contingent on many contextual and environmental variables, including the existence of an external market and the freedom to trade in that market, whether the company is vertically integrated, whether the company has an important cross-border transfer pricing activity, and the degree of divisional involvement or participation over key decision-making issues that affect their results.

No external intermediate market

An external market may not exist for the intermediate commodity, because of market monopoly, special design features of the product, patent and brand regulations, or vertical integration. This implies that all the production of that commodity is consumed internally and thus, there is total dependence on internal procurement. In other words, if the intermediate product is an essential component of the final product, the transferee division is at the "mercy" of the transferor division, which acts as a monopolist. Similarly, if the transfer product is the only or most important product to the transferor, the latter will be at the mercy of its internal buyer, which may be the only buyer, i.e. a monopsonist. The availability of alternative situations may, therefore, influence who might be identified as the principal or the private information holder.

Problems may arise because there is no market price to guide the pricing of transfers and, therefore, the transfer price is not externally verifiable. Full cost plus mark-up may be used to approximate a market price, but there is the risk of passing on inefficiencies from the selling to the buying division, especially if actual costing is used. Problems also arise if the transferor division has excess production capacity, i.e. total internal demand is less than the division's production capacity, as the excess cannot be sold externally. This has repercussions on key policies such as stock control and relationships with the suppliers, labour costs and policies, and overheads. The principal may be defined as the division having superior information. Given the lack of a market price, the transferor's intimate knowledge of costs, production schedules, etc., suggests a "principal" position. However, given the importance and frequency of the internal transaction, conflict is likely to be manifest if the dependent division is not cocooned from the impact of the TPS on its results. None the less, the dependent division may find itself in a strong bargaining position if it possesses superior information: hence the incentive for non-disclosure or unfaithful disclosure. A similar case to this is when there is an external market but divisions are prevented from trading in it.

External market exists but external sourcing is restricted

When an intermediate market exists, it may still not be reliable because of some imperfection such as political instability, economic recession, price volatility, lack of required product quality or product characteristics, reliability of delivery, etc. Moreover, even if a reliable market exists, company policy may put total or partial restrictions on external sourcing, especially when the make-or-buy decision is a strategic issue that affects the survival of the company. Stated otherwise, central management imposes barriers to entry to the external market on the divisions. As with the previous case of no external market, all or most of the production of the intermediate product is consumed internally, and thus there is great dependence on internal procurement. Bearing in mind the importance and frequency of the internal transaction, the TPS–PMERS paradox is explicit and equilibrium may be difficult to attain. Such a situation does not seem to encourage voluntary or truthful information disclosure. Again the transferor division may be the only possessor of relevant financial information.

Similar to the previous situation, problems may arise in the form of manifest and latent conflict, information impactedness, a "winner takes all" attitude, etc. None the less, the existence of an external market makes a big difference here, in that the transferee division can refer to some independent external price information, thereby countervailing the transferor's information. The market price can be used to set the internal price, depending on whether the selling division operates at or below capacity, i.e. whether there are opportunity costs attached to the internal transaction. Ultimately, pressure may be brought on the centre in order to remove or at least ease the restrictions on external sourcing. The elimination of the "barriers to entry" results in the no-restrictions case, which is discussed next.

External market exists and no sourcing restrictions

This is the ideal case of complete autonomy and no central interference in the transfer trade, especially if the external market is competitive.

Divisions have the freedom to transact either inside or outside the company and to negotiate the transfer pricing schemes among themselves. This points to the importance of divisional autonomy or the agent's participation in facilitating the equilibrium between diverging interests and the minimisation of agency costs. Although the internal transaction is important in volume terms, the transferred product is usually a standard product that requires no specific investments and thus is easily obtainable in the external market. It is also unlikely that the transfer product represents the only or the major activity of either party to the internal transaction. Examples include products whose patents have expired and which are now manufactured by companies other than the original inventor, and products in the late stages of their life cycle. This implies that market prices are readily available to serve as a basis for pricing the transfers. The market price may be adjusted for savings on external transaction costs, such as advertising and transportation costs. However, disagreements may arise between divisions over non-price aspects of the internal transaction, such as the quality of the product or service, timeliness of the transfer, etc.

The freedom of action afforded by divisional managers in this case makes the identification of either one as a principal or agent not worth while. The important relationship is between the centre and divisional management in general and whether or not the PMERS and perceived reward scheme generates an atmosphere of inter-divisional competitiveness or cooperation. The significance of this element of the control system cannot be overstated because in this case, divisional management are not only able to affect their own profit performance but that of the company also, as shown in the example below.

Example: The Genius Company Unlimited

The Genius company is a multi-divisional company whose main activity is the manufacture and sale of scientific pocket calculators. Division A makes the calculators and transfers them to Division B at £17 each. It sells the rest to external customers at £20. Other relevant information is given below.

EXAMPLE 6.1

Cost and revenue data for Genius Unlimited for the first quarter, 1994

Division A		*Division B*	
Direct materials:	£7	Variable cost	£3 per unit

Direct labour	£4	Fixed costs for first quarter	£25,000
Variable manufacturing overhead	£2	Selling price	£25 each
Variable selling	£1		
Unit variable cost	£14		
Fixed costs for the first quarter	£55,000		
Total production	40,000		
External sales	15,000		

Division B can now obtain the same quality calculators from an outside supplier at £15 each. Since there are no sourcing restrictions, Division B can either get the product from Division A or from the external supplier. Concerned about his division's financial performance, the manager of Division B is attracted by the lower purchase price from the outside supplier. Example 6.2 shows both divisional and corporate results at a transfer price of £17 per calculator.

EXAMPLE 6.2

Buying internally @ £17 per calculator

		Division A £	Division B £	Company £
Sales:	External @ £20	300,000	625,000	925,000
	Internal @ £17	425,000		
	Total sales revenue	725,000	625,000	925,000
Less:	Variable costs:			
	★ incurred	560,000	75,000	635,000
	★ transfer cost		425,000	
	Total variable costs	560,000	500,000	635,000
	Contribution margin	165,000	125,000	290,000
Less:	Fixed costs	55,000	25,000	80,000
	Profit	110,000	100,000	210,000

If the intermediate product is purchased externally at £15 and Division A cannot find an alternative customer for the internal sale, the effect on divisional and company results will be as shown in Example 6.3.

EXAMPLE 6.3

Buying externally @ £15 per calculator

		Division A £	Division B £	Company £
Sales:	External @ £20	300,000	625,000	925,000
	Internal @ £17			
	Total sales revenue	300,000	625,000	925,000
Less:	Variable costs:			
	★ incurred	210,000	75,000	285,000
	★ external purchases		375,000	375,000
	Total variable costs	210,000	450,000	660,000
	Contribution margin	90,000	175,000	265,000
Less:	Fixed costs	55,000	25,000	80,000
	Profit	35,000	150,000	185,000

Division B's action to buy externally at £15 reduces both Division A's and the company's profits. This shows that transfer pricing is not always a zero-sum game. One possible solution to this case is to get the divisions, with or without central intervention or arbitration, to negotiate the transfer price. If an agreement is made for a price of £15, the financial position of Division A and the company will improve, without affecting the results of Division B (Example 6.4).

EXAMPLE 6.4

Buying internally @ £15 per calculator

		Division A £	Division B £	Company £
Sales:	External @ £20	300,000	625,000	925,000
	Internal @ £15	375,000		
	Total sales revenue	675,000	625,000	925,000
Less:	Variable costs:			
	★ incurred	560,000	75,000	635,000
	★ transfer cost		375,000	
	Total variable costs	560,000	450,000	635,000
	Contribution margin	115,000	175,000	290,000
Less:	Fixed costs	55,000	25,000	80,000
	Profit	60,000	150,000	210,000

The decision to buy internally or externally will, undoubtedly, depend on comparing internal and external terms of the transaction, the quality of the product and the service, the long-term reliability of the service, and so on. This implies that the choice of the internal intermediate market over the external market is made on the basis of private information possessed by the particular division. Given the freedom that divisions have over decisions, it may seem that there is no apparent reason for withholding or impacting private information. However, if one adheres to the agency theory motto of motivation by self-interest to avert the risk inherent in the PMERS, a divisional manager may withhold some or all of his private information in order not to miss the best sourcing opportunity, be it internal or external. This may be especially true when inter-divisional agreements are reached to apply for some time into the future, e.g. a quarter or a year. This leads us to discuss the need for different incentives in the transfer pricing agency.

Incentives for disclosure

The main outcome of the foregoing discussions is that the transfer pricing problem is situation-specific and thus requires situation-specific solutions. It is a problem with inherent difficulties under the best of circumstances. The TPS is sought to serve many conflicting corporate and divisional objectives, some of which are financial and quantitative, while others are motivational and qualitative. In addition, it is a behavioural problem in nature which was once described by Seed (1970) as an "emotional problem", because the human factor is central to the solution finding exercise. By attempting to identify which division may be classified as the principal or agent, based on the availability of private information, it is apparent that in certain situations, the "agent" division will invariably feel disadvantaged and the merits of applying profit-centre responsibility can be openly questioned. Given the characteristics of human behaviour (e.g. bounded rationality, opportunism, etc.), one can unreservedly say that the optimum solution to the transfer pricing agency will, at best, be a compromise solution. This assertion is supported by the diversity of transfer pricing practice described in Chapter 3. Moreover, the elegance of mathematical programmes that abound in the transfer pricing literature could not achieve the much-desired "cure-all" or universal solution. Accordingly, any attempt to (over) rationalise the problem will be of no avail. In what follows, three factors are considered the vital incentives for disclosure that will achieve the compromise solution. These are:

1. divisional participation in the decision-making process;
2. the reduced reliance on accounting performance measures or APM;
3. the reward structure.

The role of participation

The necessity of participation or active involvement of divisional managers in decisions - and in particular transfer pricing decisions – derives from the existence of the performance measurement, evaluation and reward system (PMERS) usually with a budgetary control system in the background. The setting of rules to monitor the delegated responsibilities and the subsequent reward or punishment aim at constraining the behaviour of the divisional manager (or agent) taking actions that fail to further the principal's objectives. The budgetary system reflects well the agency relationship, since the budget can be considered as a contract that outlines the expectations of the principal and the agent.

Given the remoteness of the centre in the large M-form company from the operating divisions and the unobservability of managerial effort whose outcome can at best be imperfectly monitored, the constrained divisional manager may indulge in skilful manipulation of information in order to achieve a satisfactory alignment of private and social costs and benefits. Moreover, as the existence of internal trade and transfer pricing obscures the responsibility boundaries, participation has a cognitive role, in that it may increase goal and task clarity for the agent. Some of the existing empirical evidence on the positive effect of participation on performance can be related to situations of interdependence. For example, the study by Govindarajan (1984) shows that participation contributes to performance in the presence of high uncertainty; in our case, significant internal trade. The positive interaction between participation and performance is also supported by empirical evidence (Brownell, 1982) when there is heavy reliance on accounting performance measures.

Referring back to the different transfer pricing scenarios outlined earlier, the required degree of divisional participation to achieve the compromise solution depends on the availability of an external intermediate market and the importance and specificity of the internal transaction. The first and second scenarios may be eliminated from the discussion as the transfer pricing problem does not arise or the TPS-PMERS does not exist. However, if the zero or negligible internal trade results from a corporate strategy of total subcontracting which the divisions find detrimental to their operations, then the consultation with the divisions concerned over the make-or-buy decision becomes a necessity.

The remaining two scenarios present strong cases for divisional involvement. In scenario 3, where the one-off transaction is material and may impede the normal activity of the division and results in the possible loss of normal business, or requires extra non-rewarding effort, the divisional manager who is not involved or at least consulted over the decision to accept the order his division is asked to execute may resort to undesirable protective measures. The obvious reason is that the divisional manager is better placed to know about the operating and market conditions of his division and, if consulted about the special order, may suggest better alternatives that bear both short- and long-term rewards to the company and the division alike. Certainly no divisional manager would want to invest in specialised equipment which would have no rewarding alternative use once the one-off order is completed. When the internal trade is significant and recurring, as depicted in the fourth scenario, the need for participation is all too obvious. This is particularly the case if there is no external market, or if there are restrictions on external sourcing and the effects of the TPS on results are not eliminated when evaluating divisional performance. The absence of participation may create the risk that divisional managers with task interdependence and sharing rewards indulge their common interests and personal relationships and enter into overt or covert collusion, at the expense of corporate interests.

There is a risk that collusion may take place regardless of the level of internal trade, for example if managers are free to negotiate among themselves the terms of the transaction. Although negotiated transfer prices are advocated in theory, negotiation is not always conducive to narrowing the gap between conflicting interests. Motivated by self interest to limit the risk inherent in the outcome of the PMERS, the negotiating divisional manager may withhold some or all of his private information in order to influence the outcome of the bargaining process (Radner, 1985). Such behaviour is based on the prior knowledge of the rules of the bargaining process and is not necessarily motivated by desire for financial gain only. Factors like quality, reliability of supply, specificity of product and availability of substitutes, quality of service and amount of risk in transaction can all affect the behaviour of the negotiating divisional managers and may or may not contribute to the agency problems and costs.

Reducing the reliance on accounting performance measures (APM)

Divisional performance evaluation is a distinguishing feature of the decentralised company, especially the M-form company. The PMERS facilitates the control and co-ordination of divisional operations in a way that should align divisional interests with corporate objectives. This is usually done by designing accounting-based PMERS with a strong profit orientation. Accounting performance measures (or APM) include absolute profit figures: return on investment or capital employed (ROI, ROCE); residual income (RI); return on sales (ROS); and variance reports. The role of accounting information in monitoring the agent's action has been the focus of much of the contingency and agency research in accounting (Kren and Liao, 1988; and Banker, Dattar and Maindiratta, 1988). Accounting measures are incomplete aggregate measures of performance and focus on short-term outcomes rather than efforts. Moreover, much of the current debate on the obsolescence of management accounting systems in the wake of technological change, place emphasis on the inadequacy of APM to reflect key success factors (Johnson and Kaplan, 1987; Kaplan and Norton, 1992; and Cooper and Kaplan, 1991). The necessity to design balanced PMERS that combine quantitative, qualitative, financial and non-financial performance indicators has become a major concern for companies as they became more aware of the importance of strategic issues for competing in global markets. The "goal set" of any company simply cannot be translated by an aggregate accounting performance indicator (Ezzamel and Hart, 1987; Emmanuel, Otley and Merchant, 1990; Kaplan and Norton, 1992). For instance, Kaplan and Norton (1992) propose what they call a "balanced score-card" of financial and operating measures.

The behavioural implications of APM are well documented in the literature on management control (Solomons, 1965; Hopwood, 1974; Otley, 1987). The emphasis on the short-term financial performance indicator indirectly neglects the human factor because managerial effort should be considered on a long-term basis. In other words, APM do not reflect the long-term results of the agents' current efforts. In two separate studies on the relationship between environmental uncertainty and APM, Govindarajan (1984) and Brownell (1982) found that less reliance on APM for assessing subordinates' performance was necessary when uncertainty is high. Divisional interdependence creates a special type of task uncertainty, given the opposite signs of the transfer price in the objective functions of the transacting divisions. Given the TPS–PMERS paradox and excessive reliance on APM, divisional managers may feel insecure because their efforts in achieving the results are not properly considered and rewarded. As a consequence, they may indulge in what they see as legitimate and rational economic behaviour, though it may be perceived as undesirable by corporate management. The reward structure is therefore an important contingent variable for the equilibrium of the interests of the principal and the agent.

Reward structure

Participation in decision making and less reliance on APM can be expected to align conflicting interests only if they are supported by a fair reward structure. Managerial compensation is generally considered the primary solution to the agency problem as incentives aim at efficiency by eliciting the private information of divisional managers. It is argued that a properly designed compensation package would assure managers acting in the principal's interests (Rappaport, 1983). Compensation schemes – which are part of the PMERS – include both incentives and deterrents and are both pay-offs to the parties of the agency contract. The question, therefore, is how to make the incentives appeal to the risk-neutral or effort-averse agents, particularly if the TPS–PMERS paradox is consequential.

The answer lies first in the choice of the appropriate transfer pricing policy and its regular review and adjustment to accommodate changes. The choice of a transfer price should be made keeping in mind the impact on divisional results and rewards. Another important element to consider is the time the divisional manager has been in and is likely to stay in the job, as new managers are less familiar with the performance evaluation and reward system and may exhibit more caution than their peers. A manager whose contract is about to expire and who is thinking of a job change may be indifferent to the results of the PMERS.

As to the reward itself, many methods have been proposed in the literature on compensation. For instance, Philippakis and Thompson (1970) suggested basing rewards on divisional output which is tied to a budget profit level instead of actual profits. Relative performance evaluation is favoured by others (e.g. Magee, 1986) with the belief that agents who are set or pitted against their peers are better informed than the principal to monitor each other's effort. To alleviate the problem of traceability caused by interdependence, Pursell (1980) and Harris, Kriebel and Raviv (1982) opted for rewards based on corporate rather than divisional results. This last suggestion implies that, because of uncertainty and information asymmetry, the incentive scheme must induce a proper risk-sharing of the uncertain outcome (Amershi and Cheng, 1990).

SYNOPSIS

Information asymmetry naturally exists in the large company but divisional managers may not be motivated to disclose their private and superior information unless they perceive satisfaction of their self-interests. When there are linkages between organisational units in the form of internal trade and transfer prices, task uncertainty increases because responsibility boundaries become obscured.

The non-disclosure problem – which may nurture organisational conflict – may be aggravated unless there is a proper choice of transfer pricing and performance evaluation and reward policies, as well as well-structured communication channels. In addition, depending on the particular transfer pricing situation, different degrees of agent participation should be considered to attenuate the TPS–PMERS paradox in order to bring the principal–agent contractual relationship into equilibrium. The next chapter looks at different aspects of transfer pricing conflict and how it may contribute to equilibrium between incompatible goals.

QUESTIONS

1. Using the precepts of the principal–agent model, by means of a diagram illustrate and explain the agency relationships for a "real" company of your choice with three interdependent divisions. Assume different transfer pricing scenarios.
2. Extend your diagram and analysis by adding an international division located in a high corporate tax country.
3. Use your discussion in 1. and 2. above to constructively critique the principal–agent model. Outline the limitations of the PAM and suggest areas for improvement.
4. Using the Genius Company example in the text, assess the consequences on both divisional and corporate results of (i) buying internally at £16, and £19; (ii) buying externally at £14, £16, and £17. Assume that Division A prefers to sell at £17.
5. Discuss the behavioural consequences of the different transfer pricing policies in 4. above, making explicit the role of negotiation and central intervention.
6. Help top management of Genius achieve their objectives by proposing alternative incentives for private information disclosure. You may make use of the information in the diagram you drew in 1. above.
7. Compare the incentive proposals of 6. above to the alternative of eliminating divisional information manipulation through a total elimination of internal trade. You may assume that the transfer commodity has a strategic importance in the company's value chain.
8. What are the implications of these various alternatives, that is allowing through to eliminating internal trade, for the company's management accounting and control systems?

7

Conflict and Learning

INTRODUCTION

It was established in the previous chapter that the existence of internal trade and transfer prices can lead to friction between the parties to the internal transaction, and between divisions and the centre because of the effects of the transfer pricing system on divisional results and rewards. Stated otherwise, transfer pricing can be a major source of organisational conflict, yet transfer prices have been introduced into decentralised business firms to play an integrative role of the diverging interests of principals and agents in the hierarchy. Hence the study of transfer pricing conflict needs to be considered in order for the design of optimum incentive schemes to align the diverging interests of agents and principals, especially in the presence of private superior information.

DEFINITION AND TYPES OF CONFLICT

Conflict is said to arise whenever interests collide, i.e. whenever one party perceives that another party undermines some of its interests (Morgan, 1986; Huczynski and Buchanan, 1991). Conflict is a state of mind, because the divergence of interests has first to be perceived by the parties involved and it is then expressed in the form of disagreements or differences that reflect incompatibilities of interests. It is also a social process, because it involves individuals and groups (Walton and Dutton, 1969; Rahim, 1986). Moreover, it can be the result of a personality clash or it can be structurally derived and, in both cases, it manifests itself

114

through the behaviour of the people who form the organisation. The M-form company can be considered as having the potential for structural conflict, as divisional managers are implicitly encouraged to committing themselves to their objectives. This pushes them to become competitive with one another, sometimes resulting in friction and sub-optimal behaviour.

The concern in this chapter is with structural or intra-organisational conflict generated by the existence of internal trade and transfer prices. This specific context makes conflict a multidimensional relative phenomenon which evolves in episodes. It may be only felt or perceived (i.e. covert or latent), or openly manifest (i.e. overt), and may or may not have antecedents. When it is manifest it may be total or partial, and it may be simultaneous or sequential. In any case, conflict may be intended to be dysfunctional, or only for drawing attention. Therefore, the importance and the interpretation of a conflict situation depends on the causes or reasons that give rise to the conflict and a proper understanding of the people directly involved.

The managerial ambiguity inherent in the decentralised company (Vancil, 1978) and the complexities of the transfer-pricing problem described in the previous chapter indicate that conflict naturally exists in these circumstances. Hence one can presume that transfer pricing situations make conflict management more appropriate than an outright attempt to eliminate it, especially when the TPS–PMERS paradox is paramount. Transfer pricing conflict involves at least the interaction of two divisions accountable to the same head office. Recognising the potential influence of conflict is, therefore, essential for a comprehensive discourse on transfer pricing.

INTERDEPENDENCE, TRANSFER PRICING AND CONFLICT

The large hierarchical company can be described as a set of systems of simultaneous competition and collaboration which involve people with diverse interests and skills. In other words, it is a coalition in which influence processes play an important role. On the one hand, people must collaborate in pursuit of common organisational goals, yet they have to compete for limited resources, status and career advancement. The performance evaluation system plays a decisive role in this competition. Therefore, conflict is about power and politics in the hierarchy (March, 1988). Power in the M-form company can be measured by the degree of divisional autonomy over decisions, or the degree of independence in achieving outcomes. This encompasses control over resources, including information. This is sometimes referred to as "boundary management" or "boundary control" (Pfeffer, 1981, and Victor, 1990) since the quest for autonomy requires control of the division's boundary transactions. Conflict is thus inevitable in complex organisations characterised by information asymmetry and divergence of interests.

The literature on organisational behaviour identifies interdependence – whereby the actions of one division affect those of others – as one of the major sources of conflict because one party may feel that its own major goals are being blocked or interfered with, i.e. its control over its boundary transactions is blurred or curtailed. As explained in the previous chapter, interdependence creates various degrees of task ambiguity and uncertainty. Thompson's (1967) typology of pooled, sequential and reciprocal interdependence is frequently referred to in assessing intra-company conflict (Rahim, 1986; and Mills and Murgatroyd, 1991). According to Thompson, the level of conflict increases with the degree of interdependence. Conflict is at a minimum when there is little divisional interaction (pooled interdependence), but increases when the output of one division becomes the input of another division (sequential interdependence), and peaks when the outputs of divisions become the inputs of each other (reciprocal interdependence). An example of high interdependence is a vertically integrated company where backward and forward integration results in large regular volumes of intracompany transfers. It should, however, be added that if pooled interdependence involves divisions desperately competing for a scarce resource, this can also give rise to high levels of conflict over the sharing-out of the resource and the corresponding overhead costs.

NATURE OF THE TRANSFER PRICING CONFLICT

Transfer pricing is one common formal form of interdependence and resource allocation characterised as perplexing (Camman, 1929); extremely complex (Heuser, 1956; Gunn, 1981; and Farmer and Herbert, 1982); thorny (Cook, 1955; and Dearden, 1964); and puzzling (Vancil, 1978; and Eccles, 1985a). Transfer pricing reflects a managerial strategy for co-ordinating the interdependence of supposedly autonomous operating units in a non-market situation, or a simulated market within the organisation. This makes transfer pricing an emotional problem (Seed, 1970) because it creates dependence which reduces individuals' freedom and power, and is thus recognised as having a major conflict potential (Cyert and March, 1963; Hirshleifer, 1964; Watson and Baumler, 1975; Lambert, 1979; Brooke, 1984; and Knowles and Mathur, 1985). For transfer pricing conflict to become manifest, disagreements must occur between at least two divisional managers or one divisional manager and central management.

Transfer pricing conflict involves disagreements about both means and objectives, due to the cause–effect relationship between transfer pricing and divisional performance. The cause–effect relationship can also be extended to corporate results, as transfer pricing is not always a zero-sum game and, therefore, the conflict can occur between central management and divisional management. For the sake of convenience, the vertical conflict between a division and the centre will be referred to as Level One conflict, and the horizontal conflict between divisions as Level Two conflict. A third level may also be added, for conflict within divisions.

The conflict about means comes from disagreements on the transfer price itself (cost vs. market), profit mark-up, the way the transfer price is determined (mandated or negotiated), the volume and frequency of transfers, asset specificity of the intermediate product, and the freedom of sourcing if an external intermediate market exists. The choice of the transfer pricing approach can in itself be a major source of conflict, especially for idiosyncratic or proprietary products. Most of the empirical studies conducted over the last three decades have revealed that there is no one best transfer pricing approach that serves as a panacea for all situations. In most cases the choice depends on the existence and nature of an external intermediate market and the degree of autonomy divisional managers are allowed in the choice process. In sum, the conflict over the means is essentially a conflict generated by the organisational rules that govern the internal transaction.

On the other hand, the conflict about objectives concerns the simultaneous roles assigned to the TPS. These roles include resource allocation, encouragement of entrepreneurship, competition and divisional autonomy and (profit) performance evaluation. There is obviously a certain degree of incompatibility among these objectives as no single TPS can achieve them simultaneously. For instance, a centrally imposed TPS contravenes the objectives of divisional autonomy and motivation, much cherished in the literature on decentralised management. Moreover, as the transfer price is a revenue for the transferor and a cost for the transferee, the conflict over objectives resides in the impact of the TPS on divisional results as measured and rewarded by the PMERS. This was elaborated in the previous chapter where the interface between the TPS and the PMERS was discussed from the lens of agency theory. The conflict of objectives is thus a conflict over profits and costs to the parties involved in the internal trade, i.e. it is an interest or goal conflict caused by an inequitable TPS.

Goal conflict is inextricably related to the means conflict as the transfer pricing rules directly affect the achievement or blurring of divisional and/or corporate objectives. Stated otherwise, the conflict of objectives arises because transfer pricing causes the inevitable contradiction between accountability for profit (i.e. control by the centre) and the responsibility felt for profit (i.e. self control by divisional general managers), particularly when the internal trade is significant and material and divisional autonomy is curtailed. The extent of both the conflict over means and the conflict over objectives depends on the characteristics of the particular transfer pricing scenario as explained below.

Boundary management under different transfer pricing scenarios

The role of boundary management in transfer pricing conflict was first emphasised by Dean (1957), who argued that clear divisional demarcation lines were an essential requirement for effective performance measurement. Dean suggested the following four economic tests to define profit centre boundaries:

1. operational independence of the division;
2. unrestricted access to sources and markets;
3. separable divisional costs and revenues;
4. managerial intent to operate as a profit centre.

In reality, only the fourth test may hold but it may be hindered by any or all of the first three tests above. The technology, the organisational structure, the product market, and the market position of the company all impact on the type and magnitude of internal trade. Drawing clear demarcation lines, therefore, is not always possible. Since Dean's concern in proposing these criteria was with effective performance measurement, the outcome of the tests depends on the significance of the internal trade and the causal relationship between the TPS and the PMERS as detailed below.

The conflict-free scenarios

Without prejudice to the widely held view expressed earlier that conflict is inevitable in hierarchical organisations, it may be hypothesised that divisional interdependence does not always give rise to conflict. Examples of conflict-free situations are:

1. when there is no internal trade;
2. when interdependence is pooled;
3. when divisional autonomy over market choice is not constrained;
4. when transfer prices are excluded from divisional profit calculations.

The first three cases do not normally warrant elaborate transfer pricing arrangements and, consequently, are less susceptible to conflict, as explained below.

No internal trade

The simplest situation is, as argued in the previous chapter, when internal trade does not exist and transfer pricing is not a management control issue. The question to ask here, however, is whether the non-existence of conflict justifies the status quo so that there is a valid excuse for not introducing transfer pricing even if internal trade becomes a strategic issue. For instance, would it be in the best interests of a manufacturing company to subcontract a highly unique new product just for the sake of avoiding the conflict that a TPS might generate? Such a company faces the dilemma of eroding what might be a good competitive edge by divulging its technology through subcontracting, or protecting its invention through internal trade and transfer pricing, at the risk of creating a conflict situation which hitherto did not exist. Although the answer to this question requires an empirical investigation of why companies introduce transfer pricing in the first place, the trade-off in the above dilemma depends on attitudes to risk and whether corporate culture encourages organisational development and learning.

Pooled interdependence

A possibly conflict-free case is the one described by Thompson (1967), when interdependence is pooled so that there is only a negligible amount of internal trade. This rules out any significant amount of conflict, because divisional transfer pricing frictions are minimum and, therefore, there is no particular impact on performance as the TPS–PMERS paradox does not arise. In other words, there is no ambiguity as far as divisional boundary management is concerned. However, since in pooled interdependence divisions share a common resource, such as a computer centre, the central allocation of common costs to divisions can give rise to Level One conflict. If we consider cost allocation as a form of transfer pricing (Horngren and Foster, 1991), and knowing that there is always a degree of arbitrariness in cost allocation (Kaplan and Atkinson, 1989), then Level One conflict can take place when the allocated costs erode a division's profits. The relationship between cost allocation and managerial behaviour is succinctly treated by Zimmerman (1979) using the principal–agent theory.

External intermediate market exists; no sourcing restrictions

Conflict may exist in this situation but not in significant amounts as the freedom to trade internally or externally reduces the likelihood of disagreements. If, for example, there is a lack of internal customer satisfaction concerning non-price aspects such as quality and on-time delivery, the transferee has the alternative of buying the same product on the open market. The existence of the external market smoothes out internal frictions. This, of course, assumes market perfection, or near perfection, which is not always the case. The existence of an intermediate market does not necessarily mean the competitor's product is similar or at least perfectly substitutable to the internal product, nor does it guarantee favourable prices. If the external market does not offer favourable transacting terms, then Level Two conflict may arise, as one division may find itself unwillingly bound to source internally. For instance, a division may have total freedom of sourcing but prefer to buy from a sister division because the external competitor only offers a low price but does not satisfy the required quality requirements. A conscientious divisional manager may be unwilling to buy cheap quality inputs, as the apparent saving in the purchase price will manifest itself later in production line stoppages, material usage variances, final product rejects, customer complaints and decrease in sales. Alternatively, the profit-motivated manager may ignore these issues and buy cheap quality inputs externally indicating that freedom of sourcing is not a guarantor of optimum behaviour in the short term.

Transfer prices excluded from divisional profit calculations

There are two possible ways to alleviate the problem of traceability caused by interdependence and to minimise the potential of conflict, especially in companies where key decisions are centralised. The incentive scheme should provide for the impact of the TPS on divisional results, or the company should adopt company-based rather than division-based PMERS. Both methods exclude transfer prices from divisional profit calculations in order to cocoon divisional results and encourage divisional cooperation. Although it is often argued that better-informed monitoring would result if rewards were based on corporate rather than divisional results (Pursell, 1980, and Harris, Kriebel and Raviv, 1982), this raises the question of uniformity and fairness. Divisions may not be of the same size, nor be allocated the same amounts of scarce resources and, therefore, divisional contributions to overall results are not uniform and should be rewarded differently. In this case, conflict minimisation may be achieved through discretionary incentives.

The conflict-vivid scenarios

All levels of transfer pricing conflict can be expected to arise, though with varying intensity, when internal trade is considered significant by one or more divisions. In this case, interdependence and transfer pricing become a strategic issue for the company and the divisions. Divisional managers are expected to adopt strategic positions in their pursuit of boundary control. Their attitudes toward conflict depend on the strategic alternatives available to them regarding the outcomes of the TPS for their respective divisions and the flexibility of the PMERS. If maximising profits is the sole business objective, with the consequence of an emphasis on short-term oriented accounting performance measures, then clear divisional demarcation lines are not possible to draw. Let us elaborate these points further by re-examining the possible cases outlined in the preceding chapter.

Significant but non-recurring internal trade

A moderate to high level of internal trade may take place within a company on an *ad-hoc* basis – for example, to compensate for an unexpected failure in the regular external market source. If the product involved in the one-off internal transaction is a standard or regular product that would not require any special production arrangements, then conflict should not be expected to arise if the transacting terms are respected by both the transferor and the transferee. In this case it may even be possible to avoid using transfer pricing at all, thus eliminating its conflict potential. But if we assume that the transferor division is operating at capacity and the transfer transaction is imposed on it by central management so that it has to forgo established business, then both Level One and Level Two conflict can be expected to occur.

The degree of conflict may increase if the transfer transaction requires special production arrangements, such as investing in specific assets. For example, suppose that after the transferor division made the special arrangements and started working on the one-off internal order, the buying division discovers a better outside supplier and refuses to proceed with the internal deal. Whether central management intervenes or not to enforce the terms of the internal transaction, both levels of conflict will be manifest. If prevented from outsourcing, the transferee manager who normally deals in the external market and for whom the transaction may be very significant, would find it difficult to accept unfavourable internal transacting terms. If the internal transaction is not consummated, the effect may even be worse on the transferor division, given that its normal activity has been disrupted, and given its need to recoup the investment in special assets.

Significant and recurring internal trade with no external market

The repetitive nature of significant and recurring internal trade implies continuous or multi-period divisional interaction, thus increasing the chances of divisional disagreements over both means and objectives. This is where the interface between the TPS and the PMERS plays a decisive role in the aggravation or appeasement of both levels of conflict. Whether the TPS–PMERS interface would heighten and nurture conflict depends on divisional power over boundary transactions, especially in the absence of an external intermediate market.

It was stated in the previous chapter that external intermediate markets do not always exist, implying total dependence on the internal market for the procurement of the intermediate product or service. The main source of conflict resides in treating divisions as autonomous profit centres, without discounting the effect of the TPS on divisional results. Judging divisions on their profit performance requires setting the transfer at full cost plus mark-up. The absence of an external market makes the transfer price externally non-verifiable. Divisions may enter into lengthy negotiations* just to agree on the profit mark-up, especially if there is no prospect of an alternative market for either division. Divisional managers may also constantly disagree among themselves over non-price aspects of the transaction (e.g. production volume, product quality, delivery, etc.) and may enter into lengthy and resource-consuming negotiations. They may eventually ask for central intervention or arbitration.

Divisional managers may also conflict with central management if the transfer transaction is totally controlled by the centre. It should be added here that the amount and gravity of the conflict also depend on the degree of integration of the production process. When the company is highly vertically integrated, the conflict may involve all the divisions on the production sequence, especially if they are all treated as profit centres.

Whether the terms of the repetitive and significant transaction are dictated by central management or negotiated between divisions, central management may frequently need to intervene to disentangle divisional disagreements. Central intervention may, however, contribute to the existing level of conflict. If, for example, the transferor division which is treated as a profit centre is instructed to sell at full cost of, say, £10 per unit, instead of full cost plus mark-up of £15 per unit, it might resort to non-price tactics to regain its £5 profit margin. Examples of non-price tactics are a reduction in the number of parts that make the product, the use of lower quality material and labour inputs, and the reduction of quality inspection costs. All these actions affect the quality of the intermediate product, making it less and less acceptable to the transferee. If the transferee is another production division, the intermediate product will increase its product defect rate as well as its conversion costs, thus substantially eroding the profit margin. If the transferee is a marketing division, it will have obvious problems with customers. The long-term

---

*Full discussion of negotiation is left to a later section on conflict management.

effects on corporate results are easy to deduce. The denial of the £5 profit margin to the transferor division may have devastating financial and non-financial costs for the company as a whole. Hence both Level One and Level Two conflict are inevitable in the absence of an external market. Again the TPS–PMERS interface is pivotal to the analysis.

Significant and recurring internal trade with an external market

The same arguments advanced above apply when an intermediate market exists but divisions are prevented from trading in that market, either because of market imperfections or as a matter of company policy. Therefore, the imposition of "barriers to entry" to the external market and "barriers to exit" from the internal market compel divisions to stay in the internal market, even if the terms of the transfer transaction are not favourable to them. The existence of a market price for the intermediate product can be a key determinant of both the direction and the amount of conflict, as well as the conflict management strategy. Again the TPS–PMERS interface is likely to be influential in fuelling the conflict between divisional managers.

If the barriers to entry and exit are removed, one might presume that that would eradicate the potential for all levels of conflict. However, this might not always be true, given the possibility of private information manipulation by divisional managers. As argued in the preceding chapter through a numerical example, there could be a case here for Level One conflict if the transfer transaction is not zero-sum. Sub-optimal decision-making might result from divisional behaviour when autonomy of sourcing is conferred to divisions. A typical case is when a division buys from (or sells to) outside when it is in the best interest of the company as a whole to buy from (or sell to) a sister division. If corporate profitability (or performance in general) is affected, conflict ascends from Level Two to Level One. Central management may then circumvent divisional actions by controlling the sourcing and the pricing decisions. This implies that a rising level of transfer pricing conflict may adversely affect the conferral of autonomy in the decentralised company.

A GAME-THEORETIC PERSPECTIVE OF TRANSFER PRICING CONFLICT

Game theory is defined as an interactive decision theory that uses mathematical modelling for analysing conflict situations (Rasmusen, 1989; and Myerson, 1991). Any of the transfer pricing conflict scenarios described above, especially the conflict-vivid cases, comprises all the essential elements of a game, notably the players, actions, information, strategies, outcomes, pay-offs and equilibria. The players are the decision makers, who are assumed rational utility maximisers.

Given the intricacies of internal trade and the TPS–PMERS paradox, transfer pricing conflict can be characterised as a multi-facet game, which is not always zero-sum. Identification of the key players in this special type of conflict depends on the main cause of the conflict – that is, whether it is a conflict over means or objectives, and whether it is Level One or Level Two conflict.

For Level Two conflict, divisional managers will be the key players. Central management may simply be a mediator or arbitrator, i.e. a non-key player in the game, as long as overall results are not affected by divisional actions and there is no Level One conflict. Divisional actions are based on the information they possess regarding the internal transaction; the outcomes, such as quantity, quality and price; and the pay-offs they expect to derive from the alternative strategies available to them. In addition, since central management's concern is to achieve equilibrium between conflicting interests, the choice and enforcement of the compensation function can trigger Level One conflict and make central management a key player in the game.

The value placed by the divisional manager on the pay-off and, therefore, his or her behaviour to achieve the pay-off, is influenced by the TPS–PMERS interface. Moreover, both outcomes and pay-offs are influenced by the position of the player in the transfer pricing game. For instance, a monopolist transferor where no external market exists may always be the dominant player, who possesses most of the vital information and who can be very coercive in maximising his or her divisional profitability. In this case, the transfer pricing game is non-cooperative and assumes that the transferor, on top of possessing superior private information, has the ability to predict the behaviour of the transferee in the bargaining process. The transferee is an uninformed player.

The TPS–PMERS interface dictates the search for short-term equilibria which may not be easy to achieve in the decentralised company because of the non-observability of the agent's actions and the existence of information asymmetry. None the less, when the internal trade is significant and recurring, so that a long-term relationship exists, the degree of cooperation versus non-cooperation can be assessed over time through constant adjustment of the compensation function. This iterative process, called the supergame strategy (Radner, 1985), would incite the divisional manager to align his or her actions with overall interests, thus reducing the likelihood of transfer pricing conflict.

Transfer pricing conflict and learning

From a manager's perspective, conflict is a problem that requires a solution. However, the choice of solution depends very much on the way conflict is perceived and understood. The natural reaction to conflict in organisational contexts is to view it as an avoidable negative or dysfunctional force that can be attributed to some undesirable set of circumstances or causes (Morgan, 1986). This simplistic view rules out any positive effects of conflict, simply because the negative effects are usually perceived first (Notz, Starke and Atwell, 1983). This view considers that individuals, rather than bad processes or systems, are the source of conflict, and thus the aim is to reduce or eliminate conflict through some resolution procedures such as confrontation. Another perspective of conflict is to view it as an opportunity for creating positive change within a continuous learning process. For instance, Rahim (1986, p. 113) argues that organisational conflict must not necessarily be reduced, eliminated or avoided, but managed to reduce its dysfunctional outcomes and enhance its functional outcomes. Viewed in the context of the fashionable "learning organisation" concept (Handy, 1987; Garratt, 1992), transfer pricing conflict is an opportunity for creating a thinking and learning space that would facilitate divisional re-framing in a world of constant change.

When the internal transaction is of a recurring nature and, therefore, there is constant interaction and communication between divisions, it provides an important cognitive and learning platform for the people involved. For instance, transfer pricing conflict caused by the non-existence of an external market creates the opportunity for organisational development, as divisional managers who have no choice except to sell and buy from each other gradually learn to cooperate to achieve both divisional and overall objectives. This, of course, depends on top management's attitude towards conflict. It should also be added that the time-in-the-job factor (or what may be called the divisional manager's organisational life cycle) influences the individual's handling of organisational conflict. An established and well-informed divisional manager should be expected to enter into and manage conflict situations better than a newly-appointed manager. Therefore, a divisional manager's characteristics such as knowledge and experience, motivation, personality and degree of rationality, all influence the perception and handling of transfer pricing conflict.

Nevertheless, the learning experience may not always be necessarily a positive one for the organisation. Depending on the nature and importance of the internal trade, the aftermath of transfer pricing conflict resolution may have significant implications for future relations between the parties involved. Since transfer pricing involves at least two divisions, with or without central intervention, the conflict resolution procedure may result in both "winners" and "losers". A divisional manager who has now succeeded in turning the conflict to his or her advantage, based on private information manipulation, would have the incentive to behave likewise in the future in order to safeguard the present winning position. Feuding on an ongoing basis cannot be ignored as a direct repercussion.

Another example of a win–lose conflict aftermath is when central management prevents the transferee from buying the same quality intermediate product externally at a price which is cheaper than the transfer price. The legacy of the conflict situation may create the incentive for the now "losing" divisional manager to develop strategies for winning the next time round. Having "learnt a lesson", such a divisional manager may become more skilful in manipulating private information, after being involved in a series of transfer pricing wrangles.

Transfer pricing conflict management

The necessity for managing and the desirability of resolving significant transfer pricing conflict derives from the perceived dysfunctional consequences that it may inflict on the organisation. As mentioned earlier, these consequences are both financial and non-financial, and can have long-term and lasting effects. Level One and Level Two conflicts are forms of litigation that may impede corporate as well as divisional productivity, profitability and competitiveness through the loss of business opportunities. Moreover, precious management time may be continuously diverted from more important and strategic issues if significant conflict is not attended to on time. Therefore, the obvious question to ask is what strategies can be adopted to handle transfer pricing conflict?

Choice criteria for conflict management strategy

The apposite strategy may be one of many "reactive" or "proactive" strategies, but it essentially depends on the following factors:

1. the existence of antecedents;
2. the style of organisation (whether all divisions are profit centres);
3. the particular transfer pricing scenario and possible future changes to the scenario;
4. the performance measurement, evaluation and reward system (PMERS);
5. the existence of a formal body for conflict resolution;
6. the management information system;
7. the desired outcome of conflict resolution.

Past experience with any sort of organisational conflict and the legacy it might have inculcated can be a good starting point for diagnosing current situations. When there is no conflict antecedent, attention could be focused on the style of organisation because, as Spicer (1988) explains, transfer pricing conflict can be indicative of organisational inefficiency and a signal to re-examine how the interdependence is structured. This requires a full analysis of the transfer pricing scenario which gave rise to and nurtured the conflict. Particular attention should be paid to cases where there is no external market and the transaction is significant and repetitive. This is important because profit centre performance evaluation makes the incentive compensation of divisional managers a critical issue in the formulation of the apposite conflict management strategy. For instance, the results of studies by Ackelsberg and Yukl (1979) and Lambert (1979) indicate that division-based PMERS tend to be more conducive to less cooperative behaviour and to conflict than corporate-based PMERS.

If transfer pricing is part and parcel of the management control process, the success or failure experienced in the past in handling conflict can also provide sufficient evidence for the necessity of a formal conflict resolution body, if one does not already exist. Such a body may be called the Committee for Transfer Pricing Dispute Resolution. To avoid opportunistic behaviour and compartmentalised attitudes, the committee should exclude divisional managers. In handling the conflict, the committee should consider the pervasive nature of the problem in terms of its financial, non-financial, short-term, long-term, operational and strategic dimensions.

As the management information system of a company is an important characteristic of its organisational structure, transfer pricing conflict may be partly caused by inadequate communication chains. The availability, quality and timeliness of truthful financial and non-financial information can have a considerable effect on the perception and reaction of the parties involved in or concerned with a transfer pricing conflict situation. Given that information diffusion, task uncertainty and diverging interests fuel transfer pricing conflict, the need for effective communication varies with the degree of divisional interdependence. A decision support system can provide the necessary communication support and be of valuable assistance in the conflict management process. The role of decision support systems is discussed later.

Finally, the choice of the strategy should reflect the desired outcome it is expected to yield. The conflict aftermath may affect both organisation structure and goals. A conflict settlement that eliminates the profit mark-up from a full-cost-plus transfer price implies that at least one of the divisions will no longer be treated as a profit centre. Similarly, if conflict is eradicated through a total elimination of internal trade, the organisation structure of the multi-divisional company has to be redesigned. Production and marketing mix are directly affected by a change in the make-or-buy strategy.

Transfer pricing conflict management strategies

Indifference strategy

Central management may adopt an attitude of indifference to conflict, especially Level Two conflict, for at least four reasons. First, because conflict exists but is not significant and does not deserve serious attention – it is latent or covert. Second, conflict may be significant, but is not perceived as a threat to overall organisation performance. Third, central management prefers tacit and informal conflict resolution procedures, with the main aim being to use conflict as a managerial training ground. Divisional managers are deliberately left to sort out their disagreements themselves about price and non-price aspects of the internal transaction. Having been trained in the internal market, divisional managers should then be well equipped to handle external market litigations. Finally, an indifference attitude may be due to a lack of antecedents and the lack of an effective and formal conflict management system. If this is the case, the indifference strategy may lead to sub-optimum goal attainment for the divisions and the company as a whole.

Total conflict elimination strategy

The "easy" solution is to put an end to transfer pricing altogether, by eliminating all forms of commercial divisional interdependence, a strategy known as "decoupling" in the organisational literature. This is a conflict-avoidance attitude which, in terms of transaction cost analysis (Williamson, 1975, 1986), is a reversal of the initial choice of hierarchical governance structure to a market governance structure. This implies that central management perceives the savings on transaction costs (financial and non-financial) initially expected from internalising market transactions to be thwarted by the conflict. On that basis, there is no justification for keeping the internal market. Such a decision may not necessarily be in the best interest of the company at all, especially for non-standard products. It is a solution that cannot be applied to situations where a strategy of vertical integration is a prerequisite for organisational success, or where technological sensitivity requires a "make" rather than a "buy" strategy.

Alternatively, central management may adopt a policy of total conflict elimination through a dictatorship style of management, without abandoning internal trade and transfer pricing. Conflict may become forbidden, or disputes not allowed at all, so that divisional managers would only have one choice, that is, of compliance with the transfer pricing regulations. This may be adopted as a short-term solution, for example in the face of external market threats, or when there is no conflict antecedent; but it would not be a sound long-term solution for recurring and significant transfers. In addition to this, attempting a total eradication of the conflict may require committing substantial amounts of company resources, and then result in only a short-term apparent elimination of the problem. Conflict will resurface as long as internal trade and transfer pricing remain part and parcel of the company's operations.

Negotiation–arbitration strategy

The case for bargaining or negotiating was originally advocated by Cook (1955), Stone (1956), Dean (1955) and Cyert and March (1963). Negotiation is usually advocated for one of two reasons: to adjust the available market price for internal trade or in the absence of an external market, especially if there is not an adequate standard cost system. Negotiated transfer pricing in the decentralised firm is supposed to encourage autonomy, entrepreneurship and cooperation, achieve optimum corporate results, and facilitate divisional performance evaluation. The summary of surveys in Chapter 3 shows that there is ample empirical evidence to suggest that negotiated transfer pricing is common practice.

Negotiation means that the conflicting parties get together to discuss the causes of their transfer pricing disagreement and work towards an agreement. This can go through three of four phases and, in order to reach an agreement, may require concessions, compromise, collaboration or central intervention. A divisional manager may adopt different tactics, depending upon his or her position in the negotiation phases. Thus, in a transfer pricing environment, negotiation can be a double-edged sword, as it can be both a means to solving problems and a major source of conflict. Some writers, however, find negotiation to be the most defensible basis for determining transfer prices, particularly when transactions with the external environment are not viable (for instance, Cyert and March, 1963; Fremgen, 1970; and Shaub, 1978) and very promising for mitigating behavioural problems (Watson and Baumler, 1975; and Grabski, 1985). It should be pointed out here that, in addition to the transfer price, negotiation concerns all aspects of the internal transaction, including quantity, quality, investments required, delivery and frequency. Tomkins (1990) draws a further distinction between negotiating prices for all internal transactions and negotiating marginal adjustments. Negotiation can also be single- or multi-period, depending on whether transfer pricing conflict (especially Level Two conflict) is a one-off event or a recurring and embedded organisational issue.

Negotiation, on the other hand, can be time consuming and can mis-guide performance evaluation (Cook, 1955; Dopuch and Drake, 1964; and Abdel-Khalik and Lusk, 1974). When negotiation is direct and free between divisional managers, it may lead central management to evaluate managers' ability to negotiate rather than their performance itself. The ability to negotiate in itself may rest on undesirable behaviour such as gaming and data manipulation. These disadvantages reflect the conflict that divisional bargaining might generate, particularly if negotiation spans many successive periods.

Essentially, transfer pricing negotiations involve divisional managers with divergent preferences. The strategies available to each divisional manager will affect the negotiation process and its outcomes. Depending on the power of the transferor and the transferee, either division may adopt a coercive or a non-coercive strategy. Because of the TPS–PMERS interface, divisional managers' behaviour in bargaining can be very contentious. The concern about outcomes may lead to excessive divisional boundary identification, too much competition and little con-cessionary behaviour. This in turn may lead to egregious conflict and a possible stalemate as each party wants to be in a "win" position and to see its adversary in a "lose" position. These win–lose attitudes can be accentuated by divisional managers' bounded rationality and cognitive biases, the lack of relevant information and analytical tools, as well as socio-economic reasons. At the same time, central management wants to ensure that divisional bargaining yields positive motivational effects and does not impede corporate results. For instance, negotiated transfer prices cannot be allowed to reduce overall company profits, even if they may maximise divisional profits.

When divisional managers are in a "win–lose" position and are unable to agree, they will eventually turn to central management to resolve the stalemate situation. Even if divisions do not resort to central help, central management would intervene forcefully in the event of overt conflict and corporate profitability being affected. This might result in removal of profit responsibility from the buyer and seller and placing it with the chief executive (Keller, 1957; Rook, 1971). In order to preserve auton-omy in the decentralised company, the role of central management should be limited to that of a mediator or arbitrator, facilitating the nego-tiation process, as long as corporate interests are not at risk. However, if overall interests are going to be jeopardised by the contentious attitudes of divisional managers, central management will have no choice but to override divisional autonomy. An example of mediation and arbitration is to split the profit difference between the divisions so that every div-isional manager comes out of the negotiation as a winner. In this case central management avoids the "win–lose" situation and encourages a "win–win" behaviour by relaxing the TPS–PMERS interface. The win–

win strategy is one of four proactive conflict management strategies advocated by Schein (1980). A corollary of the win–win strategy is to base the PMERS on total organisational effectiveness, rather than the achievement of divisional objectives.

Another possibility is to use Hirshleifer's (1956) system of "taxes" and "bounties" to solve the problem of conflicting interests. Hirshleifer's model requires *a priori* central involvement, which contravenes divisional autonomy. Divisions are required to present their production schedules at given transfer prices. This results in a back-and-forth revision of the schedules, until an optimum is determined by central management. However, the model assumes certainty and complete and symmetrical information.

Conditions of private information and environmental uncertainty are assumed by Chalos and Haka (1990), who used a laboratory experiment in an attempt to resolve the above paradox between the autonomy of negotiating divisions and the maximisation of overall profits. Chalos and Haka examined the effect of incentive schemes, markets, and negotiation history upon decentralised transfer pricing. Essentially, they focused on the role of incentive schemes in mitigating dysfunctional consequences of negotiated transfer pricing. The results of the experiment indicated that divisional incentives – profit-based rewards – could motivate negotiators to achieve higher company profits, but did not produce greater divisional profit differences than mixed incentives (company and divisional). However, it was found that, with divisional incentives, negotiated transfer prices did not always yield optimum divisional and company results when there was market uncertainty and a short bargaining history. Instead, firm-wide incentives were observed to be most beneficial in these circumstances. Chalos and Haka concluded that the company's incentive scheme was pivotal in mitigating dysfunctional outcomes from the negotiation process. Some of these findings are similar to previous laboratory experiments by Ackelsberg and Yukl (1979) and Dejong *et al.* (1989).

Four points at least can be derived from all of the foregoing analysis. First, transfer pricing is inherently conflict-rich. Second, the misrepresentation of asymmetrical information has a major influence on the conflict and the resolution process. Third, the interface between the TPS and the PMERS is crucial to the understanding and management of conflict. Fourth, the divisional manager's organisational life cycle is vital to the manager's reaction to conflict and his behaviour during and after the conflict management process. The combination of these factors indicates that, regardless of the conflict management strategy adopted, equilibria under conditions of transfer pricing interdependence are typically inefficient. Nevertheless, one can assert that the key to alleviating the inefficiency is the PMERS through the design of suitable compensation packages. When the internal transaction is significant and repetitive, the short-term emphasis of the PMERS should be relaxed to encourage long-term divisional cooperation.

EMPIRICAL EVIDENCE ON TRANSFER PRICING CONFLICT

Very few studies of transfer pricing practice have looked at the pertinent issue of conflict. Watson and Baumler (1975) and Chalos and Haka (1990) observed that not much was known about transfer pricing conflict and the role of the accounting information system in resolving this conflict. Lambert (1979) found from a sample of US companies that the principal factor contributing to inter-divisional conflict was the financial impact of the transfer price upon a division's results. Eccles (1985b) examined the issue in thirteen American companies and found that there was a cause–effect relationship between the degree of divisional interdependence and conflict. He also observed that conflict was not necessarily a negative factor, as it was deliberately used as a management development tool in some companies. Borkowski (1990) reported that conflict was significant only between divisions, not between divisions and upper management. Negotiation was identified as the major source of conflict, noting that a greater amount of such conflict was tolerated and perhaps encouraged in setting the transfer price (Borkowski, 1990).

A recent study of domestic transfer pricing practice of thirty-three large companies in the UK by Mehafdi (1990) revealed three prime causes of conflict:

1. the importance of the transfer product to the division;
2. the impact of the transfer pricing system on divisional profits;
3. negotiation of transfer prices.

Additional results showed that for a transfer pricing policy to prevail, it had to satisfy the two criteria of fairness and conflict resolution. A mutual relationship was also found between transfer price change and conflict resolution, as in 40% of the thirty-three participating companies, transfer pricing policy change resulted in conflict reduction. It was deduced from this that the TPS can be both a source of conflict and one of the mechanisms for resolving it.

Many companies use a single conflict management procedure whereby they try to contain the conflict through encouraging collaboration (Table 7.1). In companies where there are internal barriers to entry and exit and centrally fixed transfer prices, conflict is resolved by corporate management alone. When divisional autonomy was not constrained, the

TABLE 7.1 Transfer pricing conflict management

Resolution procedure	Total[a]	Used solely
By corporate management alone	10	6
Divisions ask for revision of transfer prices	7	1
Discuss the differences openly so as to reach a compromise	14	9
Opt for mutual concessions to settle differences	5	2
Disregard the differences and emphasise common interests	3	–
Each division tries to 'win' the conflict for itself	2	1
Disputes not allowed at all	1	–
No resolution procedure exists	1	–

[a]Number of times mentioned.

most favoured resolution procedure was through dialogue or mutual problem solving.

The role of decision support systems in conflict management

It was earlier posited that the use of a decision support system – which is a computer-based system – can be instrumental in the transfer pricing conflict management process. The application of computer-based systems, in particular group decision support systems (or GDSS), in support of management decision-making has increased over the last decade or so (Nunamaker, 1989; Tanniru and Jain, 1989). Transfer pricing conflict management is a fertile ground for GDSS applications, especially computer-assisted negotiation software such as negotiation support systems (or NSS). To date there are at least six NSS software packages (Jelassi and Foroughi, 1989) which may be adapted to the transfer pricing conflict. The application of decision support systems seems more appropriate to the conflict-vivid situations described above. Freundlich (1989) outlined the merits of applying expert systems ideas to transfer pricing. Though Freundlich's system is rather primitive and does not delve into the complexities of transfer pricing, it draws attention to the potential usefulness of expert systems for the complex and contentious issue of transfer pricing.

The need for a GDSS can be justified by the simple fact that central intervention alone does not necessarily capture all the factors that give rise to and nurture the conflict. Hence, to be successful, a decision support system for transfer pricing conflict should include all the dimensions of the problem by identifying the factors that can trigger transfer pricing disagreements. These factors have already been discussed in the previous sections and can be summarised as follows:

1. number and nature of the divisions involved in the internal trade;
2. identification of common goals and divisional interests;
3. communication between divisions (and identification of semantic and syntactic differences that may lead to misunderstandings);
4. the characteristics of the internal trade (volume, frequency, type of interdependence – pooled, sequential, reciprocal);
5. the nature of the intermediate product (business importance, asset specificity and life cycle);
6. alternative transfer prices and their determination;
7. sourcing alternatives and rules;
8. the TPS–PMERS interface under different trading scenarios;
9. duration and costs of negotiations;
10. corporate versus divisional profitability under different scenarios.

It should be noted that any GDSS is only an aid to facilitate communication and achieve consensus in transfer pricing conflict situations. In essence, the GDSS acts as an integrative tool, a role that cannot be achieved if the system does not encourage the sharing of information among the parties concerned. Truthful divisional information disclosure is therefore both an aim and a challenge to the GDSS. Even if total disclosure is not achieved, the system should develop some predictive usefulness after a few successive applications. This predictive ability of the GDSS can prove useful in gauging possible changes to a present transfer pricing conflict situation if internal barriers to entry and/or to exit are introduced, reinforced or removed.

From a technical point of view, the success of the GDSS depends on the clarity and user-friendliness of the software and the adequacy of the hardware. To avoid bias and "internal computer hacking", the GDSS could be placed under the control of what was earlier called the Committe for Transfer Pricing Dispute Resolution, or any other neutral central body in the company. Finally, the decision to introduce a GDSS is a capital investment decision that requires a careful analysis of expected financial and qualitative costs and benefits. One reservation is whether the GDSS can be sufficiently versatile to accommodate the dynamics of complex transfer pricing scenarios, e.g. when imperfect and uncertain external intermediate markets exist.

SYNOPSIS

This chapter examined one important dimension of divisional interdependence: transfer pricing conflict. In order to paint an encompassing picture of this pertinent issue, two main levels of conflict were analysed, using the transfer pricing scenarios depicted in the previous chapter. As the existence of information asymmetry in the large company contributes to the principal's inability to draw first-best employment contracts, decentralisation also does not produce first-best TPS. Interdependence and transfer pricing may give rise to varying levels and degrees of conflict which cannot hastily be labelled as good or bad. It may even be said that a minimum level of conflict is necessary to encourage entrepreneurship in the decentralised company. In other words, transfer pricing conflict can be turned into a learning ground for managerial development by adopting various conflict management strategies. Computer-based decision support systems may become useful tools in transfer pricing conflict management. The TPS–PMERS interface is pivotal to the existence, the dramatisation and the management of transfer pricing conflict. Empirical evidence shows that negotiation can be both a means to solving conflict as well as one of its main causes, particularly when internal transactions are significant and the PMERS consists of divisional profit incentives.

QUESTIONS

1. Define conflict and prepare a checklist of its causes and effects for a multi-divisional company where cost allocations and transfer pricing are predominant.
2. Describe by means of a diagram, the different levels, stages and types of transfer pricing conflict for a highly vertically integrated company with four operating divisions. Assume that perfectly competitive intermediate markets exist.
3. Repeat the exercise for 2. above for a company of your choice with low to medium vertical integration.
4. Alter the diagrams in 2. and 3. above assuming that: (i) intermediate markets exist but there is a lot of uncertainty and barriers to entry, and (ii) intermediate markets do not exist.
5. Outline different conflict management strategies for the situations in questions 2. and 3. above under both market- and cost-based TPS.
6. Adapt the conflict management strategies outlined in 5. to situations 4(i) and 4(ii).
7. Suppose that you have been appointed by senior management as the official company arbitrator between conflicting divisions over transfer

pricing matters. Describe your job and outline the steps and strategies you would follow for diagnosing and resolving recurring disputes.

8. Write a short essay in which you discuss the organisational learning aspects of transfer pricing conflict.

8

Towards a Theoretical Framework

INTRODUCTION

The preceding chapters have examined the transfer pricing problem from a multi-disciplinary perspective to reflect the different dimensions of the problem, especially for the large decentralised company. It was argued that, because of the complexities of the transfer pricing issue, there was no one best TPS that can serve all situations and that decentralisation can only produce second- or third-best solutions. The aim of this chapter is to synthesise the issues and ideas developed in the preceding chapters and to propose a theoretical framework for the study of transfer pricing. The framework draws on the works of Eccles (1985a and 1985b), Spicer (1988), agency theory, contingency theory and transaction cost economics. First, a justification of the framework is proposed through an evaluation of existing models and treatments of transfer pricing which form that body of the literature that can be called "the traditional approach".

EVALUATION OF THE TRADITIONAL APPROACH

The early attempts to theorise on transfer pricing were very sporadic, with the first articles appearing in the *Journal of Accountancy* (Camman, 1929), *NACA Bulletin* (Seybold, 1935), *Economica* (Coase, 1937) and the *Accounting Review* (Broom, 1948). However, the problem came under the serious scrutiny of academics and practitioners after the

publication of articles by Cook (1955) and Dean (1955). This was followed by a more systematic approach by Hirshleifer (1956 and 1957).
The transfer pricing literature is now quite voluminous and is replete
with economic and mathematical models, accounting formulae, and
more recently, behavioural models. These are briefly reviewed below.
Elaborate syntheses of the literature can be found in Thomas (1980),
Abdel-Khalik and Lusk (1974), Grabski (1985) and McAulay and
Tomkins (1992). What is not covered by these articles, however, are
the recent works based on agency theory. These works add a useful
dimension to the interpretation and employment of contractual relationships to develop a positive theory of transfer pricing.

The economic models

Economic theory concludes that the most profitable price–output combination is the one where marginal revenue and marginal costs are equal
at the optimal output level. The economic interpretation of the transfer
pricing problem revolves around the seminal works of Hirshleifer (1956
and 1957), who modelled the problem using a marginalist approach.
Hirshleifer considered the case of a firm with only two one-product
divisions operating under a set of restrictive assumptions. Mainly, the
model assumes demand and technological independence. The aim was
to find the right transfer price at the optimum production level to maximise overall company profits, especially in the absence of a competitive
intermediate market. When such markets exist, Hirshleifer recommends
internal transacting at the intermediate market price. This proposition
finds a lot of support in the literature. If there is no market, it is assumed
that a joint level of output should be reached by the divisions so that
the buying division would handle as much output as the selling division
would produce. Thus the divisions act as quantity adjusters. The optimum transfer price is set at the selling division's marginal cost at the
optimum output level which maximises company profits. Marginal cost
pricing also applies for imperfectly competitive intermediate markets.
Thus, the most general result of Hirshleifer's model is that transfer prices
should be set at marginal costs.

Noting that Hirshleifer's basic model had a number of shortcomings –
for example, the loss of divisional autonomy and the possibility of
encouraging dysfunctional behaviour, restrictive unrealistic assumptions,
ignorance of risk and uncertainty – attempts to improve the model were
later made by Gould (1964), Ronen and McKinney (1970), Enzer
(1975), Jennergren (1972), Blois (1978), Kanodia (1979) and
Koutsoyiannis (1982). In general, the economic models deal with rather
simple cases under a set of limiting assumptions. They are based on marginal cost analysis, focus on profit maximisation, and do not preserve

divisional autonomy. The level of production and consumption as well as transfer prices are predetermined, hence the inadequacy of the resulting profits for evaluating divisional performance. Chapter 2 outlined these defects.

The inequities of the marginal approach can lead to dysfunctional behaviour, such as the manipulation of cost information by divisional managers. These limitations led to further attempts to improve the economic model through the application of mathematical modelling.

The mathematical models

Mathematical modelling extended the conceptually simpler economic models by introducing externalities – i.e. dependence between divisions – and multiple constraints into the analysis through the application of linear programming, decomposition programming and goal programming. Notable contributions include Dantzig and Wolfe (1960 and 1961), Baumol and Fabian (1964), Dopuch and Drake (1964), Samuels (1965 and 1969), Charnes et al. (1967), Salkin and Kornbluth (1973), and Bailey and Boe (1976). Demski and Krepps (1982) classify the literature in this domain into two groups. The first group focuses on imperfectly competitive markets and develops algorithms to determine transfer prices that would achieve efficient allocation of resources under capacity constraints. The second group is a recent addition to the literature as it applies the precepts of agency theory and investigates how central management could provide incentives to get divisional managers to truthfully reveal the private information they possess in order to optimise results. The contribution of agency-based transfer pricing research is discussed later. Under the programming models, transfer prices are derived from the dual values or shadow prices of the resources used. Thus the models deal with resource allocation and transfer pricing at the same time.

The mathematical models suffer from a number of problems. The iterative nature of the models requires central determination of inputs and outputs. Once the final iterations are complete, central office intervention is inevitable to stipulate divisional decisions. Divisional managers become decision executors, not decision makers. This contravenes the philosophy of decentralisation, since divisional autonomy is sacrificed for the sake of economic optimality. The iterative process could also become complex and time consuming and, as a consequence, cease to be sufficiently practical. Moreover, the complexity of the models make them administratively impractical. Apart from their mathematical elegance, the models are complicated and intractable, hence the few managerial applications in practice, as indicated in Chapter 3.

The accounting treatment

Accountants draw on the internal cost data to set transfer prices, particularly in the absence of an external intermediate market. Moreover, like the economic models and many mathematical models, the accounting approach tries to derive the transfer pricing formula that maximises company profits. Divisional managers are considered rational economic actors and are expected to be motivated so that their goals are congruent with organisational goals and culminate ultimately in profit maximisation. As with mathematical models, cost allocation and transfer pricing are "incorrigible twins" under the accounting approach. The nuance between these twins is even bigger when there is no external market for the intermediate product and the transfer price is empirically unverifiable.

A variety of solutions have been proposed by both academic and practising accountants. The basic premise for these solutions is that the transfer price represents a revenue for the selling division and a cost for the buying division. Stated otherwise, the transfer price affects divisional profitability by influencing the revenue function of the selling division and the cost function of the buying division. When there is interdependence between the production functions of two or more divisions – as under vertical integration – each division contributes to the revenue generated by the final product. The role of transfer prices is to distribute this revenue and to reflect each responsibility centre's economic contribution.

Depending on whether there is an intermediate market, the concern of the accounting approach is whether to use the market price when it is available, some formula based on internal cost data, or a combination of both, possibly involving negotiated transfer prices. The literature abounds with what can be called the "cure-all" formulae (e.g. Cook, 1955; Dean, 1955; Greer, 1962; Vendig, 1973; and Adelberg, 1986). The search for universal solutions is a direct consequence of treating transfer pricing as a mere cost–revenue exercise, devoid of its organisational and human dimensions. In contrast, many accountants acknowledge, though within the restrictive profit goal congruence assumption, that no single pricing method can satisfy all the information needs of the decentralised company (e.g. Solomons, 1965; Troxel, 1973; Sharav, 1974; Madison, 1979; Farmer and Herbert, 1982).

A SYNTHESIS OF THE TRADITIONAL APPROACH

Despite the abundance of the literature, transfer pricing remains a contentious problem for both academics and practitioners. Empirical evidence has repeatedly revealed that many of the sophisticated models and formulae developed over the last forty years or so are not appealing to practitioners, who usually prefer simplicity and ease of application to sophistication. Chapter 3 highlighted the diversity of practice, the inoperability of economic and mathematical models, and the predominance of the accounting solution. In effect, this simple and apparently naive observation conceals the very reasons why transfer pricing has persistently remained an elusive issue. The traditional approach to transfer pricing as embodied by the three models above, is in essence based on the unitary view of the firm, which is rooted in neo-classical economics. The neo-classical theory considers profit maximisation as being the sole objective of the firm, usually assuming perfectly competitive markets, rational economic actors or entrepreneurs, and a world of certainty. Previous research (e.g. Scapens and Arnold, 1986; Scapens, 1990; and Hunt and Hogler, 1990) has clearly established the link between neo-classicism and accounting research. Neo-classical models oversimplify economic reality and do not reflect the organisational and behavioural dimensions of managerial hierarchies.

Thus, there is a notable dichotomy between the traditional approach and the rationale of transfer pricing. Ironically, this rationale was clearly postulated by Hirshleifer (1964) – a pronounced neo-classical marginalist – who stated that transfer prices were not introduced into business operations as desirable innovations in their own right, but were rather the by-product of decentralisation. Decentralisation is the conscious delegation of managerial power or entrepreneurial decision making responsibility that, in return, entails accountability for outcomes in relation to allocated resources. Decentralised management is usually attributed a number of virtues, such as the enhancement of managerial decisions, development and entrepreneurship, and motivation (Thomas, 1980; Maciariello, 1984; Kaplan and Atkinson, 1989; and Emmanuel, Otley and Merchant, 1990). Divisional autonomy – in other words, the behavioural dimension – is therefore a *sine qua non* condition for decentralised management. However, the marginalist approach, by definition, does not claim to explain the behaviour of firms, but rather adapts the price mechanism to the internal market to achieve the allocation of resources that maximises short-term profits.

These observations are in fact the underlying reasons for the few behavioural and contingent studies of transfer pricing which consider organisational variables, human behaviour and environmental factors as central to the analysis and understanding of the transfer pricing problem. For instance, Whinston (1964) concluded that the marginalist approach had very little to offer for solving the transfer pricing puzzle and stated that a multi-disciplinary approach – behavioural, economic and other approaches – was the best course to follow for the derived solution to have practical managerial use. Recently, the precepts of agency theory were applied to cost allocations and transfer pricing in an attempt to explicate the paradox between the TPS and the performance evaluation and incentive schemes.

THE BEHAVIOURAL APPROACH

A pioneering work in this area is the classic organisation study by Cyert and March (1963), in which they rejected the single organisational goal of profit maximisation. Instead, they view the organisation as a coalition of participants with diverse and possibly mutually exclusive interests and objectives. The objectives can be both financial and non-financial, hence the emphasis on profit satisficing. In this context, transfer prices are the outcome of a long-run but not endless bargaining process, particularly when transactions with the external market are not viable. Conflict necessarily exists and is only partially resolved.

Negotiated transfer pricing has both advocates (e.g. Cook, 1955; Dean, 1955; Stone, 1956; Fremgen, 1970; Shaub, 1978; Watson and Baumler, 1975; and Grabski, 1985) and opponents (e.g. Dopuch and Drake, 1964; Abdel-Khalik and Lusk, 1974; Hilton, 1980; Ferguson, 1981).The latter associate conflict with dysfunctional behaviour, not as a learning process, as was discussed in Chapter 7. Prominent among the advocates of negotiated prices are Watson and Baumler (1975) who attempted an examination of transfer pricing in a behavioural setting in terms of Lawrence and Lorsch's (1967) differentiation and integration framework. Watson and Baumler asserted that if the appropriate conflict resolution process was negotiation, then negotiated transfer prices would be the best to enhance differentiation and facilitate integration. The results of a laboratory study by Ackelsberg and Yukl (1979) later indicated that negotiation resulted in more integrative and problem solving and less competitive and aggressive behaviour when divisional performance is evaluated and rewarded on corporate rather than divisional results. This view is partially refuted by Chalos and Haka (1990), who found that divisional-based incentive schemes can lead to higher company profits than mixed schemes. When private information and environmental uncertainty are taken into account, bargaining history seems to affect performance. Mixed-incentive schemes were found to be more integrative in the presence of uncertainty and short-term negotiation histories. It remains the case, however, that these contradictory results need empirical verification.

The latest extensions to the organisational approach include two important works by Eccles (1985a) and Spicer (1988) and few agency-based research papers. These developments are important in so far as the development of a comprehensive organisational model of transfer pricing is concerned.

Eccles' model

Eccles (1985a) used inductive reasoning and empirical evidence collected by means of interviews from a sample of thirteen American companies to develop a prescriptive theory to determine which transfer pricing policy should be used in practice. The theory revolves around a two-dimensional normative framework called the Managers' Analytical Plane (MAP). The two dimensions of the MAP on which transfer prices depend are (1) a strategy of vertical integration and (2) a strategy of diversification. Vertical integration indicates the degree of interdependence between responsibility centres, whereas diversification reflects the extent of product market segmentation. Eccles categorises companies into four types:

1. the collective, with low integration and diversification;
2. the competitive, with low integration and high diversification;
3. the cooperative, with high integration and low diversification;
4. the collaborative, with high integration and high diversification.

The appropriate transfer pricing policy as prescribed by the MAP is reproduced in Figure 8.1 below.

A focal point in Eccles' contingent approach is that transfer pricing depends on strategy and that a strategy of vertical integration is virtually impossible to implement without a policy of mandated internal transactions. Eccles paid particular attention to the issue of fairness of the

Vertical integration	Diversification	
	Low	*High*
High	Cooperative Mandated full cost	Collaborative Mandated market-based
Low	Collective No transfer pricing	Competitive Exchange autonomy market price

Type of organisation

FIGURE 8.1 Eccles' managers' analytical plane

TPS – or the interplay between the TPS and performance evaluation and reward – and the consequent transfer pricing conflict. Conflict was found to be used in some companies as a management style. Eccles proposed a set of thirty-eight hypotheses, some loosely phrased, and proceeded to test some of them using data from a study by Vancil (1978). Hoshower and Mandel (1986) partly tested and confirmed the validity of the MAP for twenty-five diversified American multinational companies, none of which had internal transfers of more than 10%. Thus the sample of companies is not comprehensive enough to enable an acceptable evaluation of the MAP.

Overall, Eccles' approach suffers from at least two weaknesses. Eccles was quickly dismissive of the existing accounting and economic literature, thus reducing the multi-disciplinary richness and the prescriptive content of his model (Hilton, 1980). Second he does not provide precise guide-lines or a clear paradigm as to how a firm – especially the collaborative type which is the most complex – can be positioned on the MAP. McAulay and Tomkins (1992) suggest that for Eccles' propositions to form a sound theoretical framework, they should be developed further through qualitative research and usefully combined with Spicer's (1988) more elaborate model. Eccles' (1985b) application of agency theory to the transfer pricing practices of his sample of companies is reviewed later.

Spicer's model

Spicer draws on the works of Watson and Baumler (1975), Swieringa and Waterhouse (1982), Eccles (1985a) and the growing literature on the economics of internal organisation (Williamson, 1975 and 1979) to develop an organisational model of the transfer pricing process. Spicer's model comprises a set of organisational, behavioural, strategic and transactional variables which are recognised as being susceptible to change. A particular emphasis of the model is on the situation-specificity of the internal transaction by categorising the transferred commodity as idiosyncratic, customised or standard, thus pointing to the sophistication of capital investment and sensitivity of the technology involved in the interdependent divisions. The decision to "make or buy" the intermediate product is said to hinge on the sum of production and transaction costs involved, thus reflecting the degree of exchange hazards associated with production and external procurement. Given these factors, the stability of the internal trade over time is also identified as an important dimension in the transfer pricing exercise (Figure 8.2).

A set of nine interrelated hypotheses were then proposed, and attempts to verify the validity of some of these hypotheses were recently made by Spicer and Colbert (1992), Colbert and Spicer (1992), and Emmanuel and Mehafdi (1992). Similarly to Eccles, Spicer recommends specific

Degree of transaction specific investment

Inter-divisional trade	High idiosyncratic	Neutral customised	Low standard
Stable	Manufacturing cost		
Annual change		Manufacturing cost and negotiation	
Monthly change			Market price
	No effective competition: unique properties	Differentiated in short-term	Competitive external market

FIGURE 8.2 Spicer's organisation theory model of transfer prices

transfer pricing policies to specific situations, but these still require rigorous empirical verification. Spicer rightly suggests such empirical investigation, preferably by first looking at how different business strategies affect internal trade between specific transferor and transferee centres, and then examining the similarities and/or diversity of control problems and transfer prices among them. None the less, Spicer's model should first be refined, before the empirical exercise is undertaken. While the model in its present form highlights the strategic, organisational and transactional circumstances for the choice of TPS, the important issue of divisional autonomy is not properly addressed and its dimensions are not reflected in Spicer's theory.

Agency-based models

Few attempts, including the analyses in Chapters 6 and 7, have recently been made to apply the precepts of agency theory to the study of the twin problems of cost allocations and transfer pricing. In his prize-winning article, Zimmerman (1979) demonstrated that cost allocations – which may be considered a form of transfer pricing – can be used as desirable mechanisms for motivating and controlling agents in the decentralised company. Amershi and Cheng (1990) adopt a similar approach, whereby information asymmetry is a determinant variable in intra-firm resource allocation and transfer pricing. In order to induce truthful revelation of private information, the principal (top management) is recommended to use diverse compensation schemes, which may include an incentive element (subsidy, revenue-sharing) and a deterrent element (tax, cost-sharing). Another scenario is drawn by

Yost (1990), whereby the agents have access to each other's private information more than the principal, thus assuming adverse selection. A hierarchy of equilibria is suggested, depending on which of the agents can be considered as having a dominant strategy with respect to information disclosure, especially in cases of vertical integration.

A possible alternative is the Groves' (1973) mechanism which centrally pools the benefits and costs from the internal transaction so that the fairness of the TPS is guaranteed. Radner (1985) proposes this mechanism as an alternative transfer pricing arrangement under information asymmetry. Under this mechanism, the asymmetrically informed agents are believed to have no incentive for information manipulation, as each agent is credited with the full profit of the internal transaction. The aim is to make neither division worse off than if it were trading independently. However, collusion between agents and the blurring of performance evaluation are two shortcomings of the system. Banker and Datar (1992) propose a modified version of the Groves scheme which precludes collusion. For the transfer pricing system to be immune to collusion, the agents are assumed to be risk-neutral and information asymmetry is post-contract. These are conditions that severely limit the validity of this mathematically derived model.

Eccles (1985b) built on his observations of the transfer pricing practices of thirteen American companies to identify four agency configurations whereby top management act as the principal and divisional managers the agents. Market Agency refers to situations of free market exchange with no or minimum intervention by the principal; Hierarchical Agency refers to the situation where transfer prices are centrally controlled and fixed at full cost; Conflict Agency refers to mandated market-based transfers; and Compromise Agency refers to situations of dual transfer prices. Inter-divisional conflict is found desirable if it can act as a device of mutual control between agents to ensure corporate optimality. However, the adequacy and fairness of the TPS are essential in mitigating possible dysfunctional effects of conflict. Hence Eccles emphasises the determinant role of incentive schemes and the proper design of employment contracts. Besanko and Sibley (1991) see that the formulation of compensation schemes and the determination of transfer prices under conditions of information asymmetry and moral hazard should take into account the relationship between the agent's effort and the purchased input. Both are determinants of the supplier agent's production function. However, the suggested scheme is rather ambiguous and is limited to a simplistic situation which does not reflect company practice.

The problem of information asymmetry is most critical when there is no intermediate market for the internal transaction, especially when the product is highly idiosyncratic and the internal transaction is material.

Ronen and Balachandran (1988) argue that, in the absence of an intermediate market, central management (the principal) should be cautious about disclosing information obtained from agents to each other, to avoid sub-optimal competition. This is obviously a flawed suggestion, as blocking the information does not necessarily mean that the agent had truthfully disclosed it in the first place, especially as the non-existence of an external alternative can create protectionist attitudes. This situation was discussed in detail in Chapters 6 and 7.

The extant agency-based research has at least four shortcomings. First, it seems to focus more on incorporating selected aspects of contractual relationships, like information asymmetry, moral hazard and adverse selection, into its analysis of the transfer pricing problem, rather than building coherent and comprehensive frameworks. For instance, none of the studies reviewed above make explicit the costs and benefits of transfer pricing agency and how they can be affected by alternative pricing policies. No measurements are developed to monitor costs and benefits of negotiation and different types of conflict over time, yet this is a fundamental issue in agency theory. Such measurements would affect corporate policy with regard to divisional autonomy and the design of employment contracts and incentive schemes, and enable adaptation to change. Second, none of the models questions the rationale for the existence of internal trade and transfer pricing. In other words, the available models do not investigate whether better alternatives to transfer pricing are viable at all, or whether intermittent solutions can be resorted to if an existing TPS breaks down. Third, no attempt is made to establish the relationships of agency factors with the strategic, structural and technological aspects of the problem. Finally, the research is so far essentially speculative and, apart from Eccles (1985b), no empirical verification is proposed. Hence, there is the necessity to develop what can be called an organisational framework for the study of transfer pricing that combines the traditional approach, the behavioural approach and agency-based research.

TOWARDS AN ORGANISATIONAL FRAMEWORK OF TRANSFER PRICING

When we place transfer pricing within the context of decentralisation, three issues become apparent:

1. A proper understanding and justification of internal trade should precede the search for transfer pricing policies or the design of models.
2. The search for the appropriate transfer pricing policy should first

consider the objectives to be achieved. The TPS is usually expected
to fulfil a number of conflicting objectives, not simply the maximisation of profits.
3. Consequently, the desire for objectivity or physical realism in
    accounting research (Chua, 1986) must not override the human
    and subjective (or qualitative) dimensions of transfer pricing when
    searching for solutions. Hence the need for a multi-disciplinary
    approach.

The rationale of internal trade and transfer pricing

Transfer pricing exists when there are transfers of goods and services
within the same organisational entity. Thus the existence of an intra-
organisational commercial activity, or internal trade, is a prerequisite for
transfer pricing. The empirical evidence presented in Chapter 3 indicates
that internal trade and transfer pricing are real and pervasive issues in
manufacturing industry as well as in certain service sectors. Recently,
the reorganisation of the British National Health Service led to the creation of internal markets and the introduction of transfer pricing between
clinical directorates (Ellwood, 1991; Halford, 1992). The scale of intra-
company trade is more pertinent in the international market, because of
the tax and other implications discussed in Chapters 4 and 5. The question, however, is what justifies internal trade and transfer prices, or in
Coase's (1937) terms, why are some economic activities conducted
within and not among companies?

A transaction cost economics perspective

In his seminal work on the nature of the firm, Coase posited that the
internalisation of trade is driven by transaction cost economies as multiple
market contracting is replaced by simpler and cheaper employment contracting. The costs of negotiating market contracts are an example of
costs that can be saved by internalising. Williamson (1975, 1979, and
1985) used Coase's ideas on transaction costs to develop the markets
and hierarchies model, or what is generally known as transaction costs
economics (TCE). One application of TCE to transfer pricing was that
proposed by Spicer (1988), briefly discussed earlier.

TCE views the modern organisation as an economy in miniature and
considers markets and hierarchies as alternative modes for organising
economic activity. Depending on the nature of the transaction, TCE
proposes a "governance structure" or contractual arrangement that saves
most on transaction costs. The governance structure is affected by human
factors (bounded rationality and opportunism) and environmental factors
(uncertainty/complexity and small numbers). The governance structure

also depends on whether the internal transaction involves a standard, customised, or idiosyncratic product, and the frequency or stability of the transaction. Williamson recommends that hierarchies replace markets for highly complex transactions due to higher transaction costs and external exchange hazards. This applies especially to recurring transactions of idiosyncratic products which require investments in specific human and capital assets. Empirical evidence confirms that product characteristics do affect the "make-or-buy" decision and the choice of the transfer pricing policy (Emmanuel, 1976; and Mehafdi, 1990). This is the case of technologically sensitive industries such as electronics or the patent regulated industries such as pharmaceuticals. Some companies internalise trade at all stages of production and distribution and become highly vertically integrated, usually because of technological interdependence. The aluminium industry is a typical example (Mehafdi, 1990).

A value-chain perspective

Transaction costs are not the sole justification of internal trade. The earlier quote from Hirshleifer (1964), that transfer prices are the derivatives of decentralisation – which has become a necessity for the large company because bounded rationality confines the span of control (Verlage, 1975) – implies that the essence and objectives of decentralised management and the M-form structure dictate the existence and type of transfer pricing. In other words, transfer pricing can be justified in terms of business strategy and organisational structure. McAulay and Tomkins (1992) summarise the purposes ascribed to transfer pricing in the literature into the following four overlapping sets:

1. functional necessity;
2. economic necessity;
3. organisational reasons;
4. strategic considerations.

First, functional necessity refers to the need to divisionalise companies into responsibility centres, particularly profit centres. This entails profitability measurement for divisional performance evaluation, motivation of divisional managers and international tax considerations for cross-border transfers. Second, the economic argument refers to the need to efficiently allocate scarce resources among divisions to achieve organisational goals laid out in company strategic and operational plans. Third, the role of the TPS as a tool of integration and differentiation for the divisionalised company reflects the organisational necessity. Finally, the aspect that is usually overlooked in previous research is the strategic dimension of transfer pricing. Specific transfer pricing policies are believed to be an expression of specific business strategies. The models under the traditional approach focus on some operating decisions (i.e., production but not marketing) and do not take strategic issues into account (Verlage, 1975). Hence there is an opportunity for further research, especially for investigating companies with advanced management manufacturing technology, just-in-time programmes and activity-based costing. Existing empirical evidence supports, at least partially, the contingency relationship between transfer pricing and the two determinants of strategy and structure (e.g. Eccles, 1985a; Mehafdi, 1990; Borkowski, 1990; Spicer and Colbert, 1992; and Colbert and Spicer, 1992).

In this respect, transfer pricing can be looked at using the value chain approach (henceforth VCA) proposed by Porter (1980 and 1985). As a strategy valuation tool, VCA has three distinguishing characteristics (Herbert and Morris, 1989), namely:

1. identifying the source of competitive advantage;
2. emphasising linkages within the value chain;
3. formulating generic strategies (cost leadership, differentiation and focus) to gain and sustain competitive advantage.

A firm gains competitive advantage from creating value for its customers that exceeds the cost of creating it and generates a profit. The determinants of value (e.g. low cost, sales growth and profit margin), or the value-creation ability of the firm, hinge on the two related elements of industry attractiveness and the firm's competitive position within the industry, as well as the chosen strategies for competitive positioning. VCA focuses on specific business units as sets of strategically important activities in the pursuit and sustenance of competitive advantage. This enables managers to assess which business units are creating and adding value and which are not. Non-value adding businesses can then be discontinued, subcontracted, etc., and scarce resources can thus be freed for alternative uses.

The activity set consists of activities that are freely traded in external markets and those which are not. Internal trade creates linkages of varying degrees of complexity within and between value chains of business units. Transfer pricing activities – especially the manufacture of intermediate products – may constitute a core or strategic activity sub-set that gives the company its competitive edge by creating value. For example, a company pursues and consolidates its value-creation potential through a strategy of vertical integration and internal trade. By internalising trade, the company wants to thwart and repel competitive forces such as the threat of new entrants and substitute products, by creating cost disadvantages, product differentiation, technological superiority and other barriers to entry.

VCA is a customer-driven strategy tool and its concept of value takes a different dimension when there is internal trade and transfer pricing, since there are two types of customer – internal and external – and thus two types of value. The internal customer is the transferee or transferees to whom the intermediate product is sold at the transfer price. External customers include buyers of the intermediate product at a price equal to or different from the transfer price, and buyers of final products. Therefore a transferor division is supposed to create value for both types of customer through its design, production, marketing, delivery and service activities. The transferee who is the recipient of value from the transferor is also expected to create value for the final customer. What is then the role of transfer pricing in the value chain? Does it lead to value creation, or is it just an accounting nuisance? To what extent does the value-creation ability of the transferee depend on that of the transferor? The existing VCA model does not address this aspect of value, hence the opportunity for future research, particularly for situations of high internal trade and idiosyncratic products.

In general, customers' perception of value can be different depending on their needs and the choices available to them. For instance an intermediate product can be an essential sub-assembly for the internal customer, but a final product for the external customer who retails the product without further processing. Therefore, an internal transaction does not necessarily create the same value for the internal customer as it does for the external customer. The value to the internal customer is affected by various factors, for instance the importance of the product, the existence of an intermediate market, and the locus of the pricing and sourcing decisions. The internal and external customers may pay different prices for the same intermediate product, but nevertheless the prices they pay are costs that they would like to minimise.

If the internal customer does not have freedom of sourcing and has to buy internally at a price which is higher than the available market prices for the same product, the transfer price cannot be indicative of the value-creating potential of the transferor. Since an external customer might not accept the higher price, the price difference imposed on the internal customer should be regarded as a negative value, and may reflect the transferor's inefficiencies or non-value adding activities. The internal customer, whose perception of value and therefore whose willingness to pay a certain price is driven mainly by the company's performance evaluation system, may pass on those inefficiencies to the external final customer. This reduces the value-creation ability of both the business units and the firm. In a multinational context, the manipulation of transfer prices to evade tax can also be considered as non- or negative-value creation, especially when probing by fiscal agencies and host governments incurs unwanted financial and other costs.

A suggested framework

A check-list of the interacting variables in the transfer pricing exercise can now be drawn from the preceding exposition of existing theory and empirical evidence. The check-list is then used as a basis for developing an explanatory framework which is much needed for future research (Grabski, 1985; Eccles, 1985a; McAulay and Tomkins, 1992). Seven groups of variables have been identified (Table 8.1), and their interaction is depicted in Figure 8.3 below.

Using the framework

A set of hypotheses has already been proposed by Eccles (1985a) and Spicer (1988) which can be refined and used for empirical research. The

TABLE 8.1 Check-list of interacting variables

---

1. Strategic variables
* Technology and change (AMT, JIT, ABC, value chain considerations).
* Diversification and differentiation (products and markets).
* Competitors and market positioning.
* Vertical integration.
* Subcontracting.
* Competitive advantage (cost leadership, product quality, customer satisfaction).
* Financial strategy.

---

2. Organisational structure
* Centralised vs. decentralised structure.
* Divisionalisation base (product/service; production process; regions; market served; multiple bases).
* Types of responsibility centres (cost centres; revenue centres; profit centres; investment centres; mixture).
* International subsidiaries.
* Intra-divisional structure (strategic sub-units; cost centres; etc.).
* Management information system (AIS, MAS, computer support systems).

---

3. Divisional autonomy
* Operating decisions (production, transfer prices, cost allocation, bargaining, personnel, performance measures and rewards, etc.).
* Strategic decisions (setting divisional objectives, investment decisions, make-or-buy, new products, new markets, pricing policy, etc.).

TABLE 8.1 Continued

---

4. Human variables
* Bounded rationality and opportunism.
* Leadership styles.
* Information impactedness.
* Conflict (human vs. other causes).
* Conflict management (learning and development).

---

5. Dimensions of internal trade
* Product characteristics (product design and quality, asset specificity).
* Volume significance (for company and each division).
* Frequency (stability of internal trade).

---

6. Transfer pricing system
* Objectives of TPS.
* Existence of market prices.
* Cost vs. market (single vs. multiple, dominant basis).
* Determination of profit mark-ups.
* Frequency of dominant basis (stability of transfer prices).
* Internal regulations (implicit and explicit).
* External regulations (taxation, Inland Revenue, host country).
* Locus of decision (centralised, consultation, devolved).
* Negotiation (rules, history, cost).
* Simplicity vs. complexity.
* Review and adjustment (reasons, frequency, aftermath costs vs. benefits).

---

7. Performance measurement, evaluation and reward system
* Success factors (role of strategy).
*Performance measures (accounting and non-accounting based, importance of
  profit, operating measures, short-term vs. long-term, divisional vs. company-
  wide, non-controllable factors).
* Incentive schemes (flexibility, scope, fairness, performance related pay).
* Budgetary considerations.

---

interaction of so many variables which are both quantitative and qualitative requires a team effort and a carefully drawn up research methodology.
Case-based research (Yin, 1989; and Scapens, 1990) seems to be the
most adequate in this instance, given that the typical transfer pricing
exercise can be very situation-specific. Access to data at the divisional
and sub-unit levels can be problematic, hence the choice of the research
site is important. The random selection of companies, which is usually

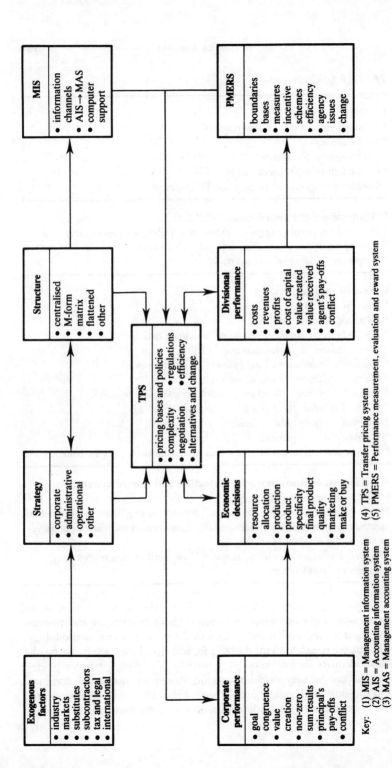

FIGURE 8.3 Causes, effects and purposes of transfer pricing

Key: (1) MIS = Management information system
(2) AIS = Accounting information system
(3) MAS = Management accounting system
(4) TPS = Transfer pricing system
(5) PMERS = Performance measurement, evaluation and reward system

done for questionnaire-based surveys to increase the statistical significance and generalisation of quantifiable results, does not suit the type
of holistic approach that the above framework requires. Therefore, the
generalisation of results should not be a prime objective for the researcher
because the very nature of the transfer pricing problem, as proven by
previous studies, does not lend itself to universality. In addition, the
subjectivity contained in many of the variables requires more than the
traditional statistical tests. Qualitative data analysis is necessary in this
exercise. Computer packages such as Ethnograph and Nudist and expert
systems can be usefully used in this respect.

SYNOPSIS

Transfer pricing is a contentious management issue, with inherent difficulties. The search for cure-all universal formulae has consumed a lot of
effort over the last four decades and has produced more questions than
it answered, particularly because of the narrowness of the neo-classical
approach. This chapter set out to synthesise the traditional approach and
to develop an encompassing explanatory framework. This framework is
not static and should be modified according to the needs of the particular
case to be investigated. Empirical work is, however, necessary to test the
validity of the model, to verify the hypotheses proposed by Eccles
(1985a) and Spicer (1988) and to develop theory. Thus, it is expected
that future research should enrich the framework for a better understanding of the transfer pricing puzzle.

QUESTIONS

1. Write a short essay in which you review and compare the different
   theories of transfer pricing.
2. Describe the influence of neo-classicism on the various transfer
   pricing models. Outline the shortcomings of these models and suggest alternatives.
3. Apply the value-chain analysis to a vertically integrated multi-
   divisional company with substantial transfers between its divisions
   of a product available in the open market. Illustrate with a detailed
   diagram.
4. Repeat the value-chain exercise for a company with a unique intermediate product. The product is shipped regularly to a subsidiary
   located in a high-tax foreign country.
5. Discuss the suggested explanatory framework and propose improvements to the cause–effect interaction between the variables.

6. Outline a research programme for a team of five researchers using the improved framework in 5. above. The team will use the project outline to apply for a two-year research grant from a professional accounting funding body. Identify companies and industries of your choice.
7. If you have used Expert Systems, develop the framework in 5. above into a knowledge-based system for teaching and/or research purposes.
8. Now that you have read this book, summarise the themes you think are critical for the design and management of a transfer pricing system for your company. Outline how you would integrate the TPS with other constituents of your management information system.

Bibliography

Abdel-Khalik, A. R. and Lusk, E. J. (1974) "Transfer pricing – a synthesis", *Accounting Review*, 49(1): 8–23.

Abdullah, F. A. (1987) *Financial management for the multinational firm*, Hemel Hempstead: Prentice-Hall.

Accounting Standards Committee (1990) *SSAP 25: segmental reporting*. ASC.

Ackelsberg, R. and Yukl, G. (1979) "Negotiated transfer pricing and conflict resolution in organizations", *Decision Sciences*, 10, July: 387–98.

Adelberg, A. H. (1986) "Resolving conflicts in intracompany transfer pricing", *Accountancy*, V. 98, N. 1119, November, pp. 86–9.

Alchian, A. A. and Demsetz, H. (1972) "Production, information costs, and economic organization", *The American Economic Review*, 62: 777–95.

Al-Eryani, M. F., Alam, P. and Akhter, S. H. (1990) "Transfer pricing determinants of US multinationals", *Journal of International Business Studies*, 21(3): 490–525.

Amershi, A. H. and Cheng, P. (1990) "Intrafirm resource allocation: the economics of transfer pricing and cost allocations in accounting", *Contemporary Accounting Research*, 7(1): 61–99.

Ansoff, I. and McDonell, E. (1990) *Implanting strategic management* (2nd edn), Hemel Hempstead: Prentice-Hall.

Aoki, M., Gustafsson, B. and Williamson, O. E. (eds) (1990) *The firm as a nexus of treaties*, London: Sage.

Armstrong, P. and Jones, C. (1992) "The decline of operational expertise in the knowledge-base of management accounting", *Management Accounting Research*, 3: 53–75.

Arpan, J. (1972) *International intracorporate pricing: non-American systems and views*, New York: Praeger.

Arvidsson, G. (1971) *Interpriser- stryrning, motivation- resultat bedomning (Transfer prices, planning, motivation and profitability analysis)*, Stockholm (English summary in Appendix 5 in Arvidsson, 1973).

Arvidsson, G. (1973) *Internal transfer negotiations: eight experiments*, Stockholm: Economic Research Institute.

Atkin, B. and Skinner, R. (1975) *How British industry prices*, Industrial Market Research Ltd.

Atkinson, A. A. (1987) *Intra-firm cost and resource allocations: theory and practice*, Toronto: The Canadian Academic Accounting Association.

Bafcop, J., Bouquin, H. and Desreumaux, A. (1991) "Prix de cessions internes: regard sur les pratiques des entreprises françaises" ("Transfer prices: a look at the practices of French companies"), *Revue Française de Gestion*, Jan–Feb: 103–18.

Bailey, A. D. and Boe, W. J. (1976) "Goal and resource transfers in the multi-goal organization", *The Accountancy Review*, 51(3): 559–573.

Baiman, S. (1982) "Agency research in managerial accounting: a survey", *Journal of Accounting Literature*, 1: 154–213.

Baiman, S. (1990) "Agency research in managerial accounting: a second look", *Accounting, Organizations and Society*, 15(4): 341–71.

Banker, R. D. and Datar, S. M. (1992) "Optimal transfer pricing under post contract information", *Contemporary Accounting Research*, 8(2) Spring: 329–52.

Banker, R. D., Dattar, S. M. and Maindiratta A. (1988) "Unobservable outcomes and multi-attribute preferences in the evaluation of managerial performance", *Contemporary Accounting Research*, 5(1) Fall: 96–124.

Barnea, A., Haugen, R. and Senbet, L. (1985) *Agency problems and financial contracting*, Hemel Hempstead: Prentice Hall.

Barone, E. (1938) "The Ministry of Production in the Collectivist State", in F. A. Von Heyek, F. A. (ed.) *Collectivist Economic Planning*, London: Routledge.

Bartlett, S. (1981) "Transnational banking: a case of transfer parking with money", in Murray, R. (ed.).

Baumol, W. J. and Fabian, T. (1964) "Decomposition, Pricing for Decentralisation and External Economies", *Management Science*, September: 1–31.

Bavishi, V. B. and Wyman, H. E. (1980) "Foreign operations disclosures by US based and multinational corporations: are they adequate?" *International Journal of Accounting*, 16(1): 153–68.

Baxter, W. T. and Oxenfeldt, A. R. (1961) "Costing and Pricing: The cost accountant versus the economist", *Business Horizons*, 4(4): Winter: 77–90.

Bazerman, M. H. and Lewicki, R. J. (1983) (eds) *Negotiating in organizations*, London: Sage Publications.

Benke, R. L. and DonEdwards, J. (1981) *Transfer pricing: techniques and uses*, New York: NAA.

Besanko, D. and Sibley, D. (1991) "Compensation and transfer pricing in a principal–agent model", *International Economics Review*, 32(1) February: 55–68.

Bierman, H. J. (1959) "Pricing intracompany transfers", *The Accounting Review*, 34, July: 429–32.

Blois, K. J. (1978) "The pricing of supplies by large customers", *Journal of Business Finance and Accounting*, 5(3), Autumn, 367–79.

Bonini, C. P., Jaedicke, R. J. and Wagner, H. (1964) (eds) *Management Controls: New Directions in Basic Research*, Maidenhead: McGraw Hill.

Borkowski, S. C. (1988) "An investigation into the divergence of theory from practice regarding transfer pricing methods", Ph.D. Dissertation, Temple University.

Borkowski, S. C. (1990) "Environmental and organizational factors affecting transfer pricing: a survey", *Journal of Management Accounting Research*, Fall, 2: 78–99.

Borkowski, S. C. (1992) "Organisational and international factors affecting multinational transfer pricing", *Advances in International Accounting*, 5: 173–92.

Bremser, W. G. and Licata, M. P. (1991) "Making transfer pricing work for your firm", *Corporate Controller*, 4(2): 47–51,57.

Bromwich, M. and Hopwood, A. G. (eds) (1986) *Research and Current Issues in Management Accounting*, London: Pitman.

Brooke, M. Z. (1984) *Centralization and Autonomy: a Study in Organization Behaviour*, New York: Holt, Rinehart and Winston.

Broom, H. N. (1948) "A method of accounting for inter-departmental profits", *The Accounting Review*, 23(4), October, 417–20.

Brownell, P. (1982) "The role of accounting data in performance evaluation, budgetary participation and locus of control", 57(4) *The Accounting Review*, October: 766–77.

Burns, J. O. (1980) "Transfer pricing decisions in US multinational corporations", *Journal of International Business Studies*, 10(2) Fall: 23–39.

Bursk, E. C., Dearden, J., Hawkins, D. F. and Longstreet, V. M. (1971) *Financial control of multinational operations*, Financial Executive Research Foundation, USA.

Camman, E. A. (1929) "Interdepartmental profits", *Journal of Accountancy*, 48, July: 37–44.

Cats-Baril, W. L., Gatti, J. F. and Grinnell, D. J. (1988) "Making transfer pricing fit your needs", *CMA Magazine (Canada)*, June: 40–44.

Chalos, P. and Haka, S. (1990) "Transfer pricing under bilateral bargaining", *The Accounting Review*, 65(3), July: 624–41.

Chandler, A. (1962) *Strategy and Structure*, Cambridge, Mass.: MIT Press.

Chandler, A. (1977) *The Visible Hand: The Managerial Revolution in American Business*, Cambridge, Mass.: Harvard University Press.

Chandler, A. and Daems, K. (1980) *Managerial Hierarchies: Comparative Perspectives on the Rise of the Modern Industrial Enterprise*, Cambridge, Mass.: Harvard University Press.

Channon, D. (1973) *The Strategy and Structure of British Enterprise*, London: Macmillan.

Channon, D. F. (1982) "Industrial Structure", *Long Range Planning* 15(5): October, 78–93.

Chenhall, R. H. (1979) "Some elements of organisational control in Australian divisionalised firms", Supplement to the *Australian Journal of Management*, 4(1) April: 1–36.

Charnes, A., W. Clower and K. O. Kortanek (1967) "Effective control through coherent decentralization with preemptive goals." *Econometrica*, 35(2), April, 294–320.

Choi, F. D. S. and Mueller, G. G. (1978) *Introduction to Multinational Accounting*, Hemel Hempstead, Prentice-Hall.

Choi, F. D. S. and Mueller, G. G. (1979) *Essentials of Multinational Accounting: an Anthology*, University Microfilms International.

Chua, W. F. (1986) "Radical developments in accounting thought", *The Accounting Review*, October: 601–32.

Coase, R. (1937) "The nature of the firm", *Economica*, 4: 386–405.

Coates, J. B., Davies, E. W., Longden, S. G., Stacey, R. J. and Emmanuel, C. R. (1993) *Corporate Performance Evaluation in Multinationals*, London: The Chartered Institute of Management Accountants: 1–209.

Colbert, G. and Spicer, B. H. (1992) "A multi-case investigation of a theory of the transfer pricing process", working paper, Universities of Kentucky, USA, and Auckland, New Zealand.

Cole, R. T. (1991) "Proposed Section 6038A Regulations", *Tax Executive*, 43(1) Jan–Feb: 26–36.

Cook, P. W., Jr. (1955) "Decentralization and the transfer price problem", *The Journal of Business*, 28: 87–94.

Cooper, R. and Kaplan, R. S. (1991) *The Design of Cost Management Systems*, Prentice Hall International.

Cooper, W. W., Leavitt, H. J. and Shelley, M. W. (1964) *New Perspectives in organisation research*, Wiley.

Cyert, R. M. and March, J. G. (1963) *A Behavioral Theory of the Firm*, Hemel Hempstead: Prentice-Hall.

Czechowicz, I. J., Choi, F. D. S. and Bavishi, V. B. (1982) *Assessing Foreign Subsidiary Performance Systems and Practices of Leading Multinational Companies*, New York: Business International Corporation.

Dale, R. (1984) *The Regulation of International Banking*, London: Woodhead-Faulkner.

Daniels, J. D., Ogram, E. W. and Radebaugh, L. (1976) *Multinational business, environments and Operations*, Wokingham: Addison-Wesley.

Danzig, G. B. and Wolfe, P. (1960) "Decomposition principle for linear programming", *Operations Research*, 8(1), January–February, 101–111.

Danzig, G. B. and Wolfe, P. (1961) "The decomposition algorithm for linear programs", *Econometrica*, 29(4), October, 767–78.

Dean, J. (1955) "Decentralization and intra-company pricing", *Harvard Business Review* 33(4), July–Aug: 65–74.

Dean, J. (1957) "Profit performance measurement of division managers", *The Controller*, September, 25: 434–4, 426 and 449.

Dearden, A. (1964) "The case of the disputing division", *Harvard Business Review*, 42: 158–9, 167, 169, 170, 172, 174, 177 and 178.

Dejong, D., Forsythe, R., Kim, J. and Uecker, W. (1989) "A laboratory investigation of alternative transfer pricing mechanisms", *Accounting, Organisations and Society*, 14(1/2): 41–64.

Demski, J. S. and Feltham, G. A. (1976) *Cost Determination: a Conceptual Approach*. Ames, IA.: Iowa State University Press.

Demski, J. S. and Kreps, D. M. (1982) "Models in managerial accounting", *Journal of Accounting Research*, 20, Supplement: 117–48.

Dopuch, N. and Drake, D. F. (1964) "Accounting implications of a mathematical programming approach to the transfer price problem", *Journal of Accounting Research*, 2(1), Spring: 10–24.

Drumm, J. H. (1972) *Theorie und praxis der lenkung durch preise (Theory and practice of using prices for control)* (English summary in Forrester, 1977).

Drumm, J. H. (1983) "Transfer pricing in the international firm", *Management International Review*, 23(4): 32–4.

Drury, C. (1991) (ed.) Chartered Institute of Management Accountants Handbook on Management Accounting Practice, London: CIMA.

Drury, C. (1992) *Management and Cost Accounting* (3rd edn), London: Chapman and Hall.

Drury, D. H. and Bates, J. H. (1979) *Data processing charge-back systems: theory and practice,* Hamilton, Ontario: The Society of Management Accountants of Canada.

Dunning, J. H. and Pearce, R. D. (1985) *The World's Largest Industrial Enterprises 1962–1983*, London: Gower.

Dunning, J. H. and Rugman, A. M. (1985) "The Influence of Hymer's dissertation on the theory of foreign direct investment", *American Economic Review*, 75: 228–32.

Dye, R. A. (1988) "Intrafirm resource allocation and discretionary actions" [in Feltham et al., 1988, pp. 349–372].

Eccles, R. G. (1985a) *The transfer pricing problem: a theory for practice*, Lexington, Mass.:

Eccles, R. G. (1985b) "Transfer pricing as a problem of agency", (Chapter 7 in Pratt and Zeckhauser, eds).

Eden, L. (1983) "Transfer pricing policies under tariff barriers", *Canadian Journal of Economics*, 16: 669–85.

Ellwood, S. (1991) "Costing and pricing healthcare", *Management Accounting (CIMA)*, 69(10) November: 26–8.

Emmanuel, C. R. (1976) "Transfer pricing in the corporate environment", unpublished Ph.D. dissertation, Lancaster University.

Emmanuel, C. R. (1977) "Transfer pricing: a diagnosis and possible solution to dysfunctional decision making in the divisionalised company", *Management International Review*, 17(4): 45–9.

Emmanuel, C. R. and Garrod, N. W. (1992) *Segment Reporting: International Issues and Evidence*, Hemel Hempstead: Prentice Hall in association with ICAEW, pp. 1–170.

Emmanuel, C. R. and Gee, K. P. (1982) "Transfer pricing: a fair and neutral procedure", *Accounting and Business Research*, Autumn: 273–8.

Emmanuel, C. R. and M. Mehafdi (1992) "Transfer pricing: an integral part of the management control system", working paper, Universities of Glasgow and Lancaster.

Emmanuel, C. R., Otley, D. T. and Merchant, K. (1990) *Accounting for Management Control* (2nd edn.), London: Chapman and Hall.

Ezzamel, M. and Hart, H. (1987) *Advanced Management Accounting: an Organizational Emphasis*, London: Cassel.

Enzer, H. (1975) "Static theory of transfer pricing", *Naval Research Logistic Quarterly*, 22(2), 375–89.

Fama, E. F. and Jensen, M. C. (1983) "Separation of ownership and control", *Journal of Law and Economics*, 26: 301–25.

Farmer, D. H. and Herbert, P. J. A. (1982) "The dilemmas of transfer pricing", *Journal of General Management*, 7(3), Spring: 47–56.

Feltham, G. A., Amershi, A. H. and Ziemba, W. T. (1988) *Economic Analysis of Information and Contracts*, Boston, Conn.: Kluwer.

Ferguson, R. C. (1981) "Transfer pricing: selecting suitable methods", *Journal of General Management*, 55(2), March–April: 53–7.

Financial Accounting Standards Board (1976) *Financial reporting for segments of a business enterprise*, Statement of Financial Accounting Standard No. 14, Stanford, Conn.: FASB.

Finnie, J. (1978) "Transfer pricing practices", *Management Accounting (CIMA)*, 56(11), December: 494–7.

Fleischman, R. F. and Parker, L. D. (1990) "Managerial accounting early in the British industrial revolution: the Carlton company, a case study", *Accounting and Business Research*, 20(79): 211–21.

Forrester, D. A. R. (1977) *Schmalembach and After: a Study of the Evolution of German Business Economics*, Glasgow: Strathclyde Convergencies.

Fremgen, J. (1970) "Transfer pricing and management goals", *Management Accounting* (NAA), 52, December: 25–31.

Freundlich, Y. (1989) "Transfer pricing: integrating expert systems in MIS environments", *IEEE Expert*, February: 54–62.

Gardner, M. J. and Lammers, L. E. (1988) "Cost accounting in large banks", *Management Accounting*, April: 34–9.

Garratt, B. (1992) *Creating the Learning Organization*, London: Fontana.

Goold, M. and Campbell, A. (1987) *Strategies and Styles: the Role of the Centre in Managing Diversified Corporations*, Oxford: Basil Blackwell.

Gould, J. R. (1964) "Economic price determination", *Journal of Business*, January: 61–7.

Governor of the Bank of England (1973) "Multinational enterprises". Text of Address given to the Société Universitaire Européene de Recherches Financières, *Bank of England Quarterly Bulletin*: 184–92.

Govindarajan, V. (1984) "Appropriateness of accounting data in performance evaluation: an empirical examination of environmental uncertainty as an intervening variable", *Accounting, Organizations and Society*, 9(2): 125–35.

Govindarajan, V. and Ramamurthy, B. (1983) "Transfer pricing policies in Indian companies", *Chartered Accountant (India)*, 32(5), November: 296–301.

Grabski, S. (1985) "Transfer pricing in complex organizations: a review and integration of recent empirical and analytical research", *Journal of Accounting Literature*, 4, Spring: 33–75.

Granick, D. (1975) "National differences in the use of internal transfer prices", *California Management Review*, Summer, 17(4): 28–40.

Gray, S. J. and Radebaugh, L. H. (1984) "International segment disclosures by US and UK multinational enterprises: a descriptive study", *Journal of Accounting Research*, 22(1): 351–60.

Gray, S. J. and Roberts, C. B. (1989) "Voluntary information disclosure and the British multinationals: corporate perceptions of cost and benefits", in Hopwood 1989 ed.

Greene, J. and Duerr, M. G. (1970) "International transactions in the multinational firm: a survey", The National Industrial Conference Board, Management International Business, Report N. 6, New York.

Greer, H. C. (1962) "Divisional profit calculation: notes on the 'transfer rate' problem", *NAA Bulletin*, 43(11), July, 5–12.

Gunn, B. (1981) "Profit maximization versus profit optimization", *Journal of Contemporary Business*, 10(2): 113–23.

Groves, T. (1973) "Incentives in teams", *Econometrica*, 41(4): 617–31.

Halford, R. (1992) "Transfer pricing comes to Barts", *Management Accounting (CIMA)*, 70(5), May: 34, 35 and 57.

Halperin, R. M. and B. Srinidhi (1991) "US income tax transfer-pricing rules and resource allocation: the case of decentralized firms", *The Accounting Review*, 66(1), Jan: 141–57.

Handy, C. (1987) *The Age of Unreason*, London: Hutchinson.

Harris, M., Kriebel, C. H. and Raviv, A. (1982) "Asymmetric information, incentives and intrafirm resource allocation", *Management Science*, 28(6), June: 604–20.

Herbert, M. and Morris, D. (1989) "Accounting data for value chain analysis", *Strategic Management Journal*, 10: 175–88.

Heuser, F. L. (1956) "Organizing for effective intra-company pricing", *NACA Bulletin*, May: 1100–5.

Hill, C. W. L. (1985) "Internal organisation and enterprise performance: some UK evidence", *Management and Decision Economics*, 6: 201–6.

Hilton, I. (1980) "Transfer pricing", *The Australian Accountant*, 50, June: 336–8.

Hirshleifer, J. (1956) "On the economics of transfer pricing", *Journal of Business*, 29: 172–84.

Hirshleifer, J. (1957) "Economics of the divisionalised firm", *The Journal of Business*, 40: 96–108.

Hirshleifer, J. (1964) "Internal pricing and decentralized decisions", in Bonini *et al.*, (eds) (1964).

Hirst, M. K. (1981) "Accounting information and the evaluation of subordinate performance: a situational approach", *The Accounting Review*, (4), October: 171–83.

Hirst, M. K. (1983) "Reliance on accounting performance measures, task uncertainty and dysfunctional behavior: some extensions", *Journal of Accounting Research*, 21(2) Autumn: 596–605.

Hopwood, A. G. (1974) *Accounting and Human Behaviour*, London: Haymarket.

Hopwood, A. G. (1989) (ed.) *International Pressures for Accounting Change*, Hemel Hempstead: Prentice-Hall–ICAEW.

Horngren, C. T. and Foster, G. (1987) *Cost Accounting: a Managerial Emphasis* (6th edn), Englewood Cliffs, N.J.: Prentice Hall International.

Hoshower, L. B. and Mandel, L. A. (1986) "Transfer pricing policies of diversified US based multinationals", *International Journal of Accounting*, 22(1) Fall: 51–60.

Howard, K., Mostafa, A. M. and Sharp, J. A. (1982) "Current issues in transfer pricing", *Managerial Finance* 8(3–4): 1–36.

Huczynski, A. and Buchanan, D. (1991) *Organizational Behaviour* (2nd edn), Hemel Hempstead: Prentice-Hall.

Hunt, H. G. III, and Hogler, R. L. (1990) "Agency theory as ideology: a comparative analysis based on critical legal theory and radical accounting", *Accounting, Organizations and Society*, 15(5): 437–54.

International Accounting Standards Committee (1981) *IAS 14: reporting financial information of segments*, IASC.

Jelassi, M. T. and Foroughi, A. (1989) "Negotiation support systems: an overview of design issues and existing software", *Decision Support Systems*, 5: 167–81.

Jennergen, P. (1972) "Decentralisation on the basis of price schedules in linear decomposable resource-allocation problems", *Journal of Financial and Quantitative Analysis*, January: 1407–17.

Jensen, M. C. and Meckling, W. H. (1976) "Theory of the firm: managerial behavior, agency costs and ownership structure", *Journal of Financial Economics*, 3: 305–60.

Jensen, O. W. (1986) "Transfer pricing and output decisions: the dynamic interaction", *Decision Sciences*, 17, Summer: 428–36.

Johnson, H. T. (1978) "Management accounting in an early multi-divisional organization: General Motors in the 1920s", *Business History Review*, 52(4) Winter: 490.

Johnson, H. T. and Kaplan, R. S. (1987) *Relevance Lost: the Rise and Fall of Management Accounting*, Boston, Mass.: Harvard Business School Press.

Kanodia, C. (1979) "Risk sharing and transfer pricing systems under certainty", *Journal of Accounting Research*, 5(3), Autumn, 367–79.

Kaplan, R. S. (1984) "The evolution of management accounting", *The Accounting Review*, 59, July: 390–418.

Kaplan, R. S. and Atkinson, A. A. (1989) *Advanced management accounting* (2nd edn), Englewood Cliffs, N.J.: Prentice-Hall.

Kaplan, R. S. and Norton, D. P. (1992) "The balanced scorecard measures that drive performance", *Harvard Business Review*, Jan–Feb, 71–9.

Kee, Y. N. and Jeong, Y. C. (1991) "South Korea – transfer pricing rules: update on developments", *East Asian Executive Reports*, 13(1), Jan.: 8, 17–18.

Keegan, D. P. and Howard, P. D. (1988) "Making transfer pricing work for services", *Journal of Accountancy*, March: 96–103.

Keller, I. W. (1957) *Management Accounting for Profit Control*, Maidenhead: McGraw-Hill.

Kim, S. H. and Miller, S. W. (1979) "Constituents of the international transfer pricing decision", *Columbia Journal of World Business*, 14(1), Spring: 69–77.

Knowles, L. L. and Mathur, I. (1985) "Factors influencing the design of international transfer pricing systems", *Managerial Finance (USA)*, 11(2): 21–4.

Koutsoyiannis, A. (1982) *Non-price decisions: the firm in a modern context*, MacMillan, London.

Kren, L. and Liao, M. (1988) "The role of accounting information in the control of organizations: a review of the evidence", *Journal of Accounting Literature*, 7: 280–309.

Lambert, D. R. (1979) "Transfer pricing and inter divisional conflict", *California Management Review*, Summer, 21(4): 70–5.

Larson, R. L. (1974) "Decentralization in real life", *Management Accounting (NAA)*, 55, March: 28–32.

Lawrence, P. R. and Lorsch, J. W. (1967) *Organization and Environment: Managing Differentiation and Integration*, Homewood, Ill.: Richard D. Irwin.

League of Nations (1932) *Taxation of Foreign and National Enterprises: a study of the tax systems and the methods of allocation of the profits of enterprises operating in more than one country, Vol. 1.* (France, Germany, Spain, the UK and the USA), No. C73.38, Geneva.

League of Nations (1933) Taxation of Foreign and National Enterprises, Vols II and III: methods of allocating taxable. Vol IV, allocation accounting for the taxable income of industrial enterprises, No. C425, M217, Geneva.

Leitch, R. A. and Barrett, K. S. (1992) "Multinational transfer pricing: objectives and constraints", *Journal of Accounting Literature*, 11: 47–92.

Lessard, D. R. and Lorange, P. (1977) "Currency changes and management control: resolving the centralization/decentralization dilemma", *The Accounting Review*, July: 628–37.

Lin, L., Lefebvre, C. and Kantor, J. (1993) "Economic determinants of international transfer pricing and the related accounting issues, with particular reference to Asian specific countries", *International Journal of Accounting*, 28: 49–70.

Livesey, F. (1967) "The pricing of internal transfers", *The Accountant*, 157 (4828) July: 99–104.

McAulay, L. and Tomkins, C. R. (1992) "A review of the contemporary transfer pricing literature with recommendations for future research", *British Journal of Management*, 3: 101–22.

Maciariello, J. A. (1984) *Management Control Systems*, Englewood Cliffs, N.J.: Prentice Hall.

Madison, R. L. (1979) "Responsibility accounting and transfer pricing: approach with caution", *Management Accounting (NAA)*, 60, January, 25–9.

Magee, R. P. (1986) *Advanced Managerial Accounting*, London: Harper and Row.

Manchester Business School (1972) *Transfer Pricing*, Research Project No. 3.

March, J. G. (1988) *Decisions and Organizations*, Oxford: Basil Blackwell.

Mautz, R. K. (1968) *Financial Reporting by Diversified Companies*, Financial Executives Research Foundation, USA.

Mehafdi, M. (1990) "Behavioural aspects of transfer pricing in U.K. decentralised companies", unpublished Ph.D. dissertation, Thames Polytechnic, London (with the collaboration of Glasgow University).

Mepham, M. J. (1980) *Accounting Models*, Polytech Publishers.

Mepham, M. J. (1983) "Robert Hamilton's contribution to accounting", *The Accounting Review*, (1) January: 43–57.

Mepham, M. J. (1988) "The Eighteenth Century origins of cost accounting", *Abacus*, (1) March: 55–74.

Merchant, K. A. and Simons, R. (1986) "Research and control in complex organizations: an overview", *Journal of Accounting Literature*, 5: 183–203.

Milburn, J. A. (1978) International transfer in a financial accounting context, University Microfilms International Michigan.

Miller, B. L. and Buckman, A. G. (1987) "Cost allocation and opportunity costs", *Management Science*, 33(5): 626–39.

Mills, A. J. and Murgatroyd, S. J. (1991) *Organizational Rules: a Framework for Understanding Organizational Action*, Buckingham: Open University Press.

Mirrlees, J. (1976) "The optimal structure of incentives and authority within an organization", *Bell Journal of Economics*, 7: 105–31.

Monden, Y. and Nagao, T. (1989) "Full Cost-based transfer pricing in the Japanese auto industry: risk-sharing and risk-spreading behaviour", in Monden and Sakurai (eds).

Monden, Y. and Sakurai, M. (1989) (eds) *Japanese Management Accounting: a World Class Approach to Profit Management*, Cambridge, Mass., Productivity Press.

Morgan, G. (1986) *Images of Organization*, London: Sage Publications.

Mostafa, A. M., Sharp, J. A. and Howard, K. (1984) "Transfer pricing: a survey using discriminant analysis", *Omega*, 12(5): 465–74.

Murray, R. (1981) (ed.) *Multinationals Beyond the Market, Intra-firm Trade and the Control of Transfer Pricing*, Brighton: Harvester.

Myerson, R. B. (1991) *Game Theory: Analysis of Conflict*, Cambridge, Mass.: Harvard University Press.

Naert, P. A. (1973) "Measuring performance in a decentralised firm with interrelated divisions: profit centre versus cost centre", *Engineering Economist*, 18: 96–110.

National Industrial Conference Board (1967) "Inter-divisional transfer pricing", *Studies in Business Policy*, 122.

Notz, W. W., Starke, F. A. and Atwell, J. (1983) "The manager as arbitrator: conflicts over scarce resources" (in Bazerman and Lewicki, 1983).

Nunamaker, J. F. (1989) "Experience with and future challenges in GDSS", *Decision Support Systems*, 5: 115–18.

OECD (1979a) *International Investment and Multinational Enterprises: Review of the 1976 Declaration Decisions*, Paris: OECD.

OECD (1979b) *Transfer Pricing and Multinational Enterprises*, Paris: Committee on Fiscal Affairs, OECD.

OECD (1993) *Tax aspects of transfer pricing within multinational enterprises: the United States Proposed Regulations*, Paris: Committee on Fiscal Affairs on the Proposed Regulations under Section 482 IRC, OECD.

Otley, D. (1987) *Accounting Control and Organizational Behaviour*, London: Heinemann.

Parker, L. D. (1979) "Divisional performance measurement: beyond an exclusive profit test", *Accounting and Business Research*, 9(36) Autumn: 309–19.

Pascale, R. T. and Athos, A. G. (1982) *The Art of Japanese Management*, London: Penguin Books.

Pear, R. (1990) "IRS investigates foreign companies for tax cheating", *The New York Times*, February 18: 1 and 30.

Picciotto, S. (1992) "International taxation and intra-firm pricing in transnational corporate groups", *Accounting, Organisations and Society*, 17(8): 759–92.

Piper, A. G. (1969) "Internal trading", *Accountancy*, 8(910) October: 733–6.

Pfeffer, J. (1981) *Power in Organizations*, London: Pitman.

Philippakis, A. S. and Thompson, E. H. (1970) "Reward function, transfer prices and decentralization", *The Quarterly Review of Economics*, 10(1) Spring: 57–66.

Porter, M. E. (1980) *Competitive Strategies: Techniques for Analysing Industries and Competitors*, New York: Free Press.

Porter, M. (1985) *Competitive Advantage*, The Free Press.

Pratt, J. W. and Zeckhauser, R. J. (1985) *Principals and Agents: the Structure of Business*, Boston, Mass.: Harvard Business School Press.

Price Waterhouse (1984) *Transfer Pricing Practices of American Industry*, Columbus, Ohio.

Prusa, T. J. (1990) "An incentive compatible approach to the transfer pricing problem", *Journal of International Economics*, 28: 155–72.

Pursell, R. B. (1980) "Administering divisional incentive compensation", *Compensation Review*, 1: 15–20.

Radner, R. (1985) "The internal economy of large firms", *The Economic Journal*, Supplement, 96: 1–22.

Rahim, M. A. (1986) *Managing Conflict in Organizations*. New York: Praeger.

Rappaport, A. (1983) *Information for Decision-Making: Readings in Cost and Managerial Accounting* (3rd edn) Hemel Hempstead: Prentice-Hall.

Rasmussen, E. (1989) *Games and Information: an Introduction to Game Theory*, Oxford: Blackwell.

Reekie, D. and Weber, M. H. (1979) *Profits, Politics and Drugs*. London: Macmillan.

Reve, T. (1990) "The firm as a nexus of internal and external contracts", (in Aoki *et al.* (eds) 1990).

Ronen, J. (1992) "Transfer Pricing Reconsidered", *Journal of Public Economics*, 47: 125–36.

Ronen, J. and Balachandran, K. R. (1988) "An approach to transfer pricing under uncertainty", *Journal of Accounting Research* 26(2), Autumn, 300–14.

Ronen, J. and G. McKinney (1970) "Transfer pricing for divisional autonomy", *Journal of Accounting Research*, 8(1), Spring: 99–112.

Rook, A. (1971) *Transfer Pricing: a Measure of Management Performance in Multi-Divisional Companies.* British Institute of Management, management survey report No. 8.

Rumelt, R. P. (1974) *Strategy, Structure and Economic Performance*, Cambridge, Mass.: Harvard University Press.

Sacks, S. R. (1983) *Self Management and Efficiency: Large Corporations in Yugoslavia*, London: George Allen and Unwin.

Salkin, G. R. and Kornbluth, J. (1973) *Linear programming in financial planning*, London: Haymarket.

Samuels, J. M. (1965) "Opportunity costing: an application of mathematical programming", *Journal of Accounting Research*, 3(2), Autumn: 182–91.

Samuels, J. M. (1969) "Penalties and subsidies in internal pricing policies", *Journal of Business Finance*, 1(3), Autumn: 31–38.

Scapens, R. W., Cooper, D. and Arnold, J. (1983) *Management accounting research and practice.* CIMA, London.

Scapens, R. W. (1990) "Researching management accounting practice: the role of case study methods", *British Accounting Review*, 22(3): 303–21.

Scapens, R. W. and Arnold, J. (1986) "Economics and management accounting research", [in Bromwich and Hopwood (eds).]

Scapens, R. W., Sale, J. T. and Tikkas, P. A. (1982) *Financial control of divisional capital investment*, London: The Institute of Cost and Management Accountants.

Schein, E. H. (1980) *Organisational Psychology*, Hemel Hempstead: Prentice-Hall.

Seed, A. H. (1970) "The rational abuse of accounting information", *Management Accounting*, 51(7) January: 9–11.

Senn, J. A. (1990) *Information Systems in Management* (4th edn), Belmont: Wadsworth.

Seybold, R. (1935) "Some aspects of inter-unit accounting methods" *NACA Bulletin*, October, 34–46.

Shank, J. K. and Govindarajan, V. (1989) *Strategic Cost Analysis: the Evolution from Managerial to Strategic Accounting.* Homewood, Ill.: Irwin.

Sharav, I. (1974) "Transfer pricing – diversity of goals and practices", *Journal of Accountancy*, 137, April, 56–62.

Sharma, V. S. (1992) "Determining product profitability", *Bankers Magazine*, March/April: 67–71.

Shaub, J. (1978) "Transfer pricing in a decentralized organization", *Management Accounting (NAA)*, 59: 33, 36 and 42.

Shulman, J. S. (1969) "Transfer pricing in the multinational firm", *European Business*, 20, January: 46–54.

Silbertson, A. (1970) "Surveys of applied economics: price behaviour of firms", *Economic Journal*, 80: 512–82.

Sizer, J. (1979) *An Insight into Management Accounting*, London: Pitman.

Solomon, L. and Tsay, J. (1985) "Pricing of computer services: a survey of industry practices", *Cost and Management*, March–April, 59(2): 5–9.

Solomons, D. (1965) *Divisional Performance Measurement and Control*, New York: Richard D. Irwin.

Spicer, B. H. (1988) "Towards an organizational theory of the transfer pricing process", *Accounting, Organizations and Society*, 13(3): 303–21.

Spicer, B. H. (1992) "The resurgence of cost and management accounting: a review of some recent developments in practice, theories and case research methods", *Management Accounting Research*, 3: 1–37.

Spicer, B. H. and Ballew, V. (1983) "Management accounting systems and the economics of internal organization", *Accounting, Organizations and Society*, 8: 73–96.

Spicer, B. H. and Colbert, G. (1992) "The interaction of competitive strategy, organisation design, costing systems and transfer pricing in a high technology firm", working paper, Universities of Auckland, New Zealand; and Kentucky, U.S.A.

Stone, W. E. (1956) "Intracompany pricing", *The Accounting Review*, 31(4), October: 625–7.

Stone, W. E. (1973) "An early English Cotton Mill cost accounting system: Charlton Mills 1810–1889", *Accounting and Business Research*, 4(1), Winter: 71–8.

Stopford, J. H., Channon, D. F. and Constable, J. (1980) *Cases in strategic management*. Chichester, John Wiley and Sons.

Swieringa, R. J. and Waterhouse, J. M. (1982) "Organizational views on transfer pricing", *Accounting, Organizations and Society*, 7(2): 149–65.

The Sunday Times (1992) "Inland Revenue probes tax avoidance at Sony", March 22: 7 and 16.

Tang, R. Y. W. (1979) *Transfer Pricing Practices in the USA and Japan*. New York: Praeger.

Tang, R. Y. W. (1981) *Multinational Transfer Pricing: Canadian and British Perspectives*, Toronto: Butterworths and Co. Ltd.

Tang, R. Y. W. (1982) "Environmental variables of multinational transfer pricing: a UK perspective", *Journal of Business Finance and Accounting* 9: 179–89.

Tang, R. Y. W. (1992) "Transfer pricing in the 1990s", *Management Accounting*, February: 22–6.

Tanniru, M. R. and Jain, H. K. (1989) "Knowledge-based GDSS to support reciprocally interdependent decisions", *Decision Support Systems*, 5: 287–301.

Thomas, A. L. (1980) *Behavioural Analysis of Joint Cost Allocations and Transfer Pricing*, New York: Stipes Publishing.

Thompson, J. D. (1967) *Organizations in Action*, New York: McGraw-Hill.

Tiessen, P. and Waterhouse, J. H. (1983) "Towards a descriptive theory of management accounting", *Accounting, Organizations and Society*, 2(3): 581–95.

Tomkins, C. R. (1973) *Financial Planning in Divisionalised Companies*, London: Haymarket.

Tomkins, C. R. (1990) "Making sense of cost-plus transfer prices where there are imperfect intermediate good markets by a 'pragmatic-analytical' Perspective", *Management Accounting Research*, 1: 199–216.

Tomkins, C. R. and McAulay, L. (1991) "Modelling fair transfer prices where no market guidelines exist", in Drury (ed.).

Troxel, R. B. (1973) "On transfer pricing", *CPA Journal*, October: 806–7.

United Kingdom Monopolies Commission (1973) *Chlordiazepoxide and Diazepam*.

United Nations (1978) *Transnational corporations in world development: a re-examination*.

United Nations (1978) *International Standards of Accounting and Reporting Transnational Corporations*, Commission on Transnational Corporations, October.

United States Treasury and IRS (1988) *A Study of inter-company pricing*, White Paper, October.

Vancil, R. (1979) *Decentralization: Managerial Ambiguity by Design*, Homewood, Ill.: Dow-Jones-Irwin.

Vendig, R. E. (1973) "A three-part transfer price", *Management Accounting (NAA)*, 55, September: 33–6.

Verrechia, R. E. (1983) "Discretionary disclosure", *Journal of Accounting and Economics*, 5: 179–94.

Verlage, H. C. (1975) *Transfer Pricing for Multinational Enterprises*, Rotterdam, Rotterdam University Press.

Victor, B. (1990) "Co-ordinating work in complex organizations", *Journal of Organizational Behaviour*, 11(3), May: 187–99.

Walton, R. E. and Dutton, J. M. (1969) "The management of interdepartmental conflict: a model and review", *Administrative Science Quarterly*, 14, December: 522–42.

Watson, D. J. H. and Baumler, J. V. (1975) "Transfer pricing: a behavioural context", *The Accounting Review*, 50(3), July: 466–74.

Wells, M. C. (1968) "Profit centres, transfer prices and mysticism", *Abacus*, 4(2), December: 174–81.

Wheeler, J. E. (1988) "An academic look at transfer pricing in a global economy", *Tax Notes*, July 4: 87–96.

Wheeler, J. E. (1990) *Hearings on Tax Underpayments by Foreign-owned US Subsidiaries*, House Ways and Means Oversight Sub-Committee of the United States House of Representatives: 1–15.

Whinston, A. (1964) "Price guides in decentralized organizations", in Cooper *et al.*, 1964.

Whiting, E. A. and Gee, P. K. (1984) "Decentralisation, divisional interdependence and the treatment of central costs as charges or allocations", Paper presented to the 7th Annual Congress of the European Accounting Association, Saint Gallen, Switzerland, April 10–12.

Williamson, O. E. (1975) *Markets and Hierarchies: Analysis and Anti-trust Implications: a Study in the Economics of Internal Organization*, New York: The Free Press.

Williamson, O. E. (1979) "Transaction cost economics: the governance and contractual relations", *The Journal of Law and Economics*, October: 233–61.

Williamson, O. E. (1985) *The economic institutions of capitalism: firms, markets and rational contracting*, New York: The Free Press.

Williamson, O. E. (1986) *Economic organizations: firms, markets and policy control*, New York: Wheatsheaf Books.

Wright, D. T. (1992) *International Tax Summaries: a guide for planning and decisions. Coopers and Lybrand International Tax Network*, New York: Wiley and Sons.

Wu, F. and Sharp, D. (1979) "An empirical study of transfer pricing practice", *International Journal of Accounting*, 14(2), Spring: 71–99.

Yin, R. K. (1989) Case Study Research: Design and Methods, London: Sage Publications.

Yost, J. A. (1990) "Intra-firm resource allocation and transfer pricing under asymmetric information: a principal–agent analysis of decentralised decision-making in a multi-division firm", Unpublished Ph.D. dissertation, Ohio State University, USA.

Yunker, P. J. (1982) *Transfer Pricing and Performance Evaluation in Multinational Corporations: a Survey Study*, New York: Praeger.

Yunker, P. J. (1983) "A survey study of subsidiary autonomy, performance evaluation and transfer pricing in multinational corporations", *Columbia Journal of World Business*, 19, Fall: 51–64.

Zimmerman, J. L. (1979) "The Costs and Benefits of Cost Allocations", *The Accounting Review*, July: 504–21.

Index